MznLnx

Missing Links Exam Preps

Exam Prep for

Advanced Calculus

Kaplan, 5th Edition

The MznLnx Exam Prep is your link from the texbook and lecture to your exams.
The MznLnx Exam Preps are unauthorized and comprehensive reviews of your textbooks.

All material provided by MznLnx and Rico Publications (c) 2010
Textbook publishers and textbook authors do not particpate in or contribute to these reviews.

MznLnx

Rico Publications

Exam Prep for Advanced Calculus
5th Edition
Kaplan

Publisher: Raymond Houge
Assistant Editor: Michael Rouger
Text and Cover Designer: Lisa Buckner
Marketing Manager: Sara Swagger
Project Manager, Editorial Production: Jerry Emerson
Art Director: Vernon Lowerui

Product Manager: Dave Mason
Editorial Assitant: Rachel Guzmanji
Pedagogy: Debra Long
Cover Image: Jim Reed/Getty Images
Text and Cover Printer: City Printing, Inc.
Compositor: Media Mix, Inc.

(c) 2010 Rico Publications
ALL RIGHTS RESERVED. No part of this work covered by the copyright may be reproduced or used in any form or by an means--graphic, electronic, or mechanical, including photocopying, recording, taping, Web distribution, information storage, and retrieval systems, or in any other manner--without the written permission of the publisher.

Printed in the United States
ISBN:

For more information about our products, contact us at:
Dave.Mason@RicoPublications.com

For permission to use material from this text or product, submit a request online to:
Dave.Mason@RicoPublications.com

Contents

CHAPTER 1
Vectors and Matrices — 1

CHAPTER 2
Differential Calculus of Functions of Several Variables — 7

CHAPTER 3
Vector Differential Calculus — 20

CHAPTER 4
Integral Calculus of Functions of Several Variables — 27

CHAPTER 5
Vector Integral Calculus — 35

CHAPTER 6
Infinite Series — 45

CHAPTER 7
Fourier Series and Orthogonal Functions — 62

CHAPTER 8
Functions of a Complex Variable — 71

CHAPTER 9
Ordinary Differential Equations — 86

CHAPTER 10
Partial Differential Equations — 95

ANSWER KEY — 107

TO THE STUDENT

COMPREHENSIVE

The *MznLnx* Exam Prep series is designed to help you pass your exams. Editors at MznLnx review your textbooks and then prepare these practice exams to help you master the textbook material. Unlike study guides, workbooks, and practice tests provided by the texbook publisher and textbook authors, *MznLnx* gives you **all** of the material in each chapter in exam form, not just samples, so you can be sure to nail your exam.

MECHANICAL

The MznLnx Exam Prep series creates exams that will help you learn the subject matter as well as test you on your understanding. Each question is designed to help you master the concept. Just working through the exams, you gain an understanding of the subject--its a simple mechanical process that produces success.

INTEGRATED STUDY GUIDE AND REVIEW

MznLnx is not just a set of exams designed to test you, its also a comprehensive review of the subject content. Each exam question is also a review of the concept, making sure that you will get the answer correct without having to go to other sources of material. You learn as you go! Its the easiest way to pass an exam.

HUMOR

Studying can be tedious and dry. MznLnx's instructional design includes moderate humor within the exam questions on occassion, to break the tedium and revitalize the brain

Chapter 1. Vectors and Matrices

1. In mathematics and its applications, a _____ system is a system for assigning an n-tuple of numbers or scalars to each point in an n-dimensional space. This concept is part of the theory of manifolds. 'Scalars' in many cases means real numbers, but, depending on context, can mean complex numbers or elements of some other commutative ring.
   - a. 15 theorem
   - b. Spherical coordinate system
   - c. Coordinate
   - d. Cylindrical coordinate system

2. In elementary mathematics, physics, and engineering, a _____ is a geometric object that has both a magnitude (or length), direction and sense, (i.e., orientation along the given direction.) A _____ is frequently represented by a line segment with a definite direction, or graphically as an arrow, connecting an initial point A with a terminal point B, and denoted by

   >

   The magnitude of the _____ is the length of the segment and the direction characterizes the displacement of B relative to A: how much one should move the point A to 'carry' it to the point B.

   Many algebraic operations on real numbers have close analogues for vectors.
   - a. BDDC
   - b. Linear partial differential operator
   - c. Vector
   - d. 15 theorem

3. In mathematics, a _____ in a normed vector space is a vector (often a spatial vector) whose length is 1 (the unit length.) A _____ is often denoted by a lowercase letter with a superscribed caret or e;hate;, like this: $\hat{\imath}$.

   In Euclidean space, the dot product of two unit vectors is simply the cosine of the angle between them.
   - a. ALGOR
   - b. Overdetermined
   - c. Unit vector
   - d. ACTRAN

4. In mathematics, _____ is one of the basic operations defining a vector space in linear algebra Note that _____ is different from scalar product which is an inner product between two vectors.

   More specifically, if K is a field and V is a vector space over K, then _____ is a function from K × V to V. The result of applying this function to c in K and v in V is denoted cv.
   - a. Vector-valued function
   - b. Direction cosines
   - c. Homogeneous function
   - d. Scalar Multiplication

5. In mathematics, the _____ is an operation which takes two vectors over the real numbers R and returns a real-valued scalar quantity. It is the standard inner product of the orthonormal Euclidean space. It contrasts with the cross product which produces a vector result.
   - a. Homogeneous function
   - b. Vector-valued function
   - c. Scalar multiplication
   - d. Dot product

Chapter 1. Vectors and Matrices

6. In mathematics, an _____ space is a vector space with the additional structure of _____. This additional structure associates each pair of vectors in the space with a scalar quantity known as the _____ of the vectors. Inner products allow the rigorous introduction of intuitive geometrical notions such as the length of a vector or the angle between two vectors.

   a. ALGOR
   b. AUSM
   c. Inner product
   d. ACTRAN

7. In mathematics, two vectors are _____ if they are perpendicular, i.e., they form a right angle. For example, a subway and the street above, although they do not physically intersect, are _____ if they cross at a right angle.

   a. ACTRAN
   b. AUSM
   c. ALGOR
   d. Orthogonal

8. For some curves there is a smallest number L that is an upper bound on the length of any polygonal approximation. If such a number exists, then the curve is said to be rectifiable and the curve is defined to have _____ L.

   Let C be a curve in Euclidean (or, generally, a metric) space X = R^n, so C is the image of a continuous function f : [a, b] → X of the interval [a, b] into X.

   a. Integrand
   b. Integration by parametric derivatives
   c. Order of integration
   d. Arc length

9. The _____ of an angle is the ratio of the length of the adjacent side to the length of the hypotenuse. In our case

$$\cos A = \frac{\text{adjacent}}{\text{hypotenuse}} = \frac{b}{h}.$$

   The tangent of an angle is the ratio of the length of the opposite side to the length of the adjacent side. In our case

$$\tan A = \frac{\text{opposite}}{\text{adjacent}} = \frac{a}{b}.$$

   The remaining three functions are best defined using the above three functions.

   a. Trigonometric
   b. Trigonometric functions
   c. Sine integral
   d. Cosine

10. _____ is the long dimension of any object. The _____ of a thing is the distance between its ends, its linear extent as measured from end to end. This may be distinguished from height, which is vertical extent, and width or breadth, which are the distance from side to side, measuring across the object at right angles to the _____.

    a. 15 theorem
    b. BDDC
    c. BIBO stability
    d. Length

Chapter 1. Vectors and Matrices

11. In mathematics, the _____ is a binary operation on two vectors in a three-dimensional Euclidean space that results in another vector which is perpendicular to the plane containing the two input vectors. The algebra defined by the _____ is neither commutative nor associative. It contrasts with the dot product which produces a scalar result.
    a. Permutation
    b. Fundamental theorem of algebra
    c. 15 theorem
    d. Cross product

12. Someone who is _____ will prefer to use this hand for everyday activities, such as writing, maintaining personal hygiene, cooking and so forth. According to a variety of studies, anywhere from 70% to 90% of the world population is _____, while most of the remaining are left-handed. A small percentage of the population can use both hands equally well; a person with this ability is deemed to be ambidextrous (though such people may still have a personal preference of one hand over the other.)
    a. BIBO stability
    b. 15 theorem
    c. Right-handed
    d. BDDC

13. In computer science and information science, _____ could also be a method or an algorithm. Again, an example will illustrate: There are systems of counting, as with Roman numerals, and various systems for filing papers, or catalogues, and various library systems, of which the Dewey Decimal _____ is an example. This still fits with the definition of components which are connected together (in this case in order to facilitate the flow of information.)
    a. BIBO stability
    b. 15 theorem
    c. System
    d. BDDC

14. In vector calculus, there are two ways of multiplying three vectors together, to make a _____ of vectors. Three vectors defining a parallelepiped

The scalar _____ is defined as the dot product of one of the vectors with the cross product of the other two.

Geometrically, the scalar _____

$$\mathbf{a} \cdot (\mathbf{b} \times \mathbf{c})$$

is the (signed) volume of the parallelepiped defined by the three vectors given.

    a. Divergence
    b. Gradient theorem
    c. Green's theorem
    d. Triple product

15. In algebra, a _____ is a function depending on n that associates a scalar, det(A), to an n×n square matrix A. The fundamental geometric meaning of a _____ is a scale factor for measure when A is regarded as a linear transformation. Determinants are important both in calculus, where they enter the substitution rule for several variables, and in multilinear algebra.

For a fixed nonnegative integer n, there is a unique _____ function for the n×n matrices over any commutative ring R. In particular, this function exists when R is the field of real or complex numbers.

a. 15 theorem
b. BDDC
c. BIBO stability
d. Determinant

16. In several fields of mathematics the term _____ is used with different but closely related meanings. They all relate to the notion of mapping the elements of a set to other elements of the same set, i.e., exchanging (or 'permuting') elements of a set.

The general concept of _____ can be defined more formally in different contexts:

In combinatorics, a _____ is usually understood to be a sequence containing each element from a finite set once, and only once.

a. Linear combinations
b. Fundamental theorem of algebra
c. 15 theorem
d. Permutation

17. The _____ of any solid, liquid, plasma, vacuum or theoretical object is how much three-dimensional space it occupies, often quantified numerically. One-dimensional figures (such as lines) and two-dimensional shapes (such as squares) are assigned zero _____ in the three-dimensional space. _____ is commonly presented in units such as mL or cm^3 (milliliters or cubic centimeters.)

a. Klein-Gordon equation
b. Volume
c. Dirac equation
d. Vector potential

18. In mathematics, the complex numbers are an extension of the real numbers obtained by adjoining an imaginary unit, denoted i.

Every _____ can be written in the form a + bi, where a and b are real numbers called the real part and the imaginary part of the _____, respectively.

Complex numbers are a field, and thus have addition, subtraction, multiplication, and division operations. These operations extend the corresponding operations on real numbers, although with a number of additional elegant and useful properties, e.g., negative real numbers can be obtained by squaring complex (imaginary) numbers.

a. Filled Julia set
b. Complex number
c. Conjugated line
d. Real part

19. In mathematics, the _____ of a function y = f(x) is a function that, in some fashion, 'undoes' the effect of f The _____ of f is denoted f^{-1}. The statements y=f(x) and $x=f^{-1}(y)$ are equivalent.

a. Inverse
b. ACTRAN
c. AUSM
d. ALGOR

20. In discrete mathematics, the _____ is used when solving recurrence problems. One can specify a recurrence relation of the form

$$t_n = At_{n-1} + Bt_{n-2}$$

where the value of t_n is dependent on the values of t_{n-1} and t_{n-2}. When solving a recurrence relation, the goal is to eliminate this dependency and derive an equation of the form

$$t_n = c_1 r_1^n + c_2 r_2^n,$$

where c_1 and c_2 are constants and r_1 and r_2 are the roots of the _____

$$r^2 - Ar - B = 0,$$

where A and B are the constants defined in the original recurrence relation.

a. Discriminant
b. Sheffer sequence
c. Characteristic equation
d. Leading coefficient

21. In mathematics, an _____ space is a topological space whose dimension is n (where n is a fixed natural number.) The archetypical example is _____ Euclidean space, which describes Euclidean geometry in n dimensions.

Many familiar geometric objects can be generalized to any number of dimensions.

a. BIBO stability
b. BDDC
c. 15 theorem
d. N-dimensional

22. In physics, _____ is movement that changes the position of an object, as opposed to rotation. For example, according to Whittaker:

A _____ is the operation changing the positions of all points (x, y, z) of an object according to the formula

$$(x, y, z) \rightarrow (x + \Delta x, y + \Delta y, z + \Delta z)$$

where $(\Delta x, \Delta y, \Delta z)$ is the same vector for each point of the object. The _____ vector $(\Delta x, \Delta y, \Delta z)$ common to all points of the object describes a particular type of displacement of the object, usually called a linear displacement to distinguish it from displacements involving rotation, called angular displacements.

a. BDDC
b. 15 theorem
c. BIBO stability
d. Translation

23. In a totally ordered set all elements are mutually comparable, so such a set can have at most one minimal element and at most one maximal element. Then, due to mutual comparability, the minimal element will also be the least element and the maximal element will also be the greatest element. Thus in a totally ordered set we can simply use the terms minimum and _____.

a. Leibniz rule
c. Racetrack principle
b. Nth term
d. Maximum

Chapter 2. Differential Calculus of Functions of Several Variables

1. A curve γ is said to be closed or a loop if $I = [a, b]$ and if $\gamma(a) = \gamma(b)$. A _____ is thus a continuous mapping of the circle S^1; a simple _____ is also called a Jordan curve or a Jordan arc. The Jordan curve theorem states that such curves divide the plane into an 'interior' and an 'exterior'.
   a. Curve
   b. Closed curve
   c. Bullet-nose curve
   d. Kappa curve

2. In metric topology and related fields of mathematics, a set U is called _____ if, intuitively speaking, starting from any point x in U one can move by a small amount in any direction and still be in the set U. In other words, the distance between any point x in U and the edge of U is always greater than zero.

   As an example, consider the _____ interval (0, 1) consisting of all real numbers x with 0 < x < 1. Here, the topology is the usual topology on the real line. We can look at this in two ways.

   a. Open
   b. AUSM
   c. ACTRAN
   d. ALGOR

3. In mathematics, a _____ is an ordered list of objects (or events). Like a set, it contains members (also called elements or terms), and the number of terms (possibly infinite) is called the length of the _____. Unlike a set, order matters, and the exact same elements can appear multiple times at different positions in the _____.
   a. 15 theorem
   b. Y-intercept
   c. Slope
   d. Sequence

4. In mathematics, a (topological) _____ is defined as follows: let I be an interval of real numbers (i.e. a non-empty connected subset of $\mathbb{R}$); then a _____ γ is a continuous mapping $\gamma : I \to X$, where X is a topological space. The _____ γ is said to be simple if it is injective, i.e. if for all x, y in I, we have $\gamma(x) = \gamma(y) \implies x = y$. If I is a closed bounded interval $[a, b]$, we also allow the possibility $\gamma(a) = \gamma(b)$ (this convention makes it possible to talk about closed simple _____.)
   a. Prolate cycloid
   b. Tractrix
   c. Closed curve
   d. Curve

5. In mathematics, a _____ is a function for which, intuitively, small changes in the input result in small changes in the output. Otherwise, a function is said to be discontinuous. A _____ with a continuous inverse function is called bicontinuous. An intuitive though imprecise (and inexact) idea of continuity is given by the common statement that a _____ is a function whose graph can be drawn without lifting the chalk from the blackboard.
   a. Continuous function
   b. Visual Calculus
   c. Binomial series
   d. Hyperbolic angle

6. In elementary mathematics, physics, and engineering, a _____ is a geometric object that has both a magnitude (or length), direction and sense, (i.e., orientation along the given direction.) A _____ is frequently represented by a line segment with a definite direction, or graphically as an arrow, connecting an initial point A with a terminal point B, and denoted by

Chapter 2. Differential Calculus of Functions of Several Variables

The magnitude of the _____ is the length of the segment and the direction characterizes the displacement of B relative to A: how much one should move the point A to 'carry' it to the point B.

Many algebraic operations on real numbers have close analogues for vectors.

a. BDDC
b. Vector
c. Linear partial differential operator
d. 15 theorem

7. In calculus, a branch of mathematics, the _____ is a measurement of how a function changes when its input changes. Loosely speaking, a _____ can be thought of as how much a quantity is changing at some given point. For example, the _____ of the position (or distance) of a vehicle with respect to time is the instantaneous velocity (respectively, instantaneous speed) at which the vehicle is traveling.

The process of finding a _____ is called differentiation. The fundamental theorem of calculus states that differentiation is the reverse process to integration.

a. Derivative
b. Semi-differentiability
c. Bounded function
d. Stationary phase approximation

8. In infinitesimal calculus, a _____ is traditionally an infinitesimally small change in a variable. For example, if x is a variable, then a change in the value of x is often denoted Δx (or δx when this change is considered to be small.) The _____ dx represents such a change, but is infinitely small.

a. Dirichlet integral
b. Local maximum
c. The Method of Mechanical Theorems
d. Differential

9. In algebra, a _____ is a function depending on n that associates a scalar, det(A), to an n×n square matrix A. The fundamental geometric meaning of a _____ is a scale factor for measure when A is regarded as a linear transformation. Determinants are important both in calculus, where they enter the substitution rule for several variables, and in multilinear algebra.

For a fixed nonnegative integer n, there is a unique _____ function for the n×n matrices over any commutative ring R. In particular, this function exists when R is the field of real or complex numbers.

a. BIBO stability
b. 15 theorem
c. BDDC
d. Determinant

10. In mathematics, a _____ is a function with multiplicative scaling behaviour: if the argument is multiplied by a factor, then the result is multiplied by some power of this factor.

Suppose that $f : V \to W$ is a function between two vector spaces over a field F.

Chapter 2. Differential Calculus of Functions of Several Variables

We say that f is homogeneous of degree k if

$$f(\alpha \mathbf{v}) = \alpha^k f(\mathbf{v})$$

for all nonzero $\alpha \in F$ and $\mathbf{v} \in V$.

a. Dot product
b. Direction cosines
c. Direction vector
d. Homogeneous function

11. The _____ of any solid, liquid, plasma, vacuum or theoretical object is how much three-dimensional space it occupies, often quantified numerically. One-dimensional figures (such as lines) and two-dimensional shapes (such as squares) are assigned zero _____ in the three-dimensional space. _____ is commonly presented in units such as mL or cm^3 (milliliters or cubic centimeters.)

a. Volume
b. Klein-Gordon equation
c. Vector potential
d. Dirac equation

12. In mathematics, an _____ is a generalization for the concept of a function in which the dependent variable has not been given 'explicitly' in terms of the independent variable. To give a function f explicitly is to provide a prescription for determining the output value of the function y in terms of the input value x:

y = f(x.)

By contrast, the function is implicit if the value of y is obtained from x by solving an equation of the form:

R(x,y) = 0.

a. Automatic differentiation
b. Implicit differentiation
c. Ordinary differential equation
d. Implicit function

13. In mathematics and its applications, _____ refers to finding the linear approximation to a function at a given point. In the study of dynamical systems, _____ is a method for assessing the local stability of an equilibrium point of a system of nonlinear differential equations or discrete dynamical systems. This method is used in fields such as engineering, physics, economics, and ecology.

a. Differentiation of trigonometric functions
b. Parametric derivative
c. Smooth function
d. Linearization

14. In mathematics, the _____ of a function y = f(x) is a function that, in some fashion, 'undoes' the effect of f The _____ of f is denoted f^{-1}. The statements y=f(x) and x=f^{-1}(y) are equivalent.

a. ALGOR
b. AUSM
c. ACTRAN
d. Inverse

Chapter 2. Differential Calculus of Functions of Several Variables

15. In mathematics, if f is a function from A to B then an _____ for f is a function in the opposite direction, from B to A, with the property that a round trip (a composition) from A to B to A (or from B to A to B) returns each element of the initial set to itself. Thus, if an input x into the function f produces an output y, then inputting y into the _____ f^{-1} (read f inverse, not to be confused with exponentiation) produces the output x. Not every function has an inverse; those that do are called invertible.
    a. Aristotle
    b. Augustin Louis Cauchy
    c. Augustin-Jean Fresnel
    d. Inverse function

16. In mathematics, the _____ is a two-dimensional coordinate system in which each point on a plane is determined by an angle and a distance. The _____ is especially useful in situations where the relationship between two points is most easily expressed in terms of angles and distance; in the more familiar Cartesian or rectangular coordinate system, such a relationship can only be found through trigonometric formulation.

    As the coordinate system is two-dimensional, each point is determined by two polar coordinates: the radial coordinate and the angular coordinate.

    a. BDDC
    b. BIBO stability
    c. Polar coordinate system
    d. 15 theorem

17. In mathematics and its applications, a _____ system is a system for assigning an n-tuple of numbers or scalars to each point in an n-dimensional space. This concept is part of the theory of manifolds. 'Scalars' in many cases means real numbers, but, depending on context, can mean complex numbers or elements of some other commutative ring.
    a. Cylindrical coordinate system
    b. Spherical coordinate system
    c. 15 theorem
    d. Coordinate

18. A _____ is one of the most curvilinear basic geometric shapes:It has two faces, zero vertices, and zero edges. The surface formed by the points at a fixed distance from a given straight line, the axis of the _____. The solid enclosed by this surface and by two planes perpendicular to the axis is also called a _____.
    a. Right circular cylinder
    b. BDDC
    c. Cylinder
    d. 15 theorem

19. If a particular point on a sphere is (arbitrarily) designated as its _____, then the corresponding antipodal point is called the south pole and the equator is the great circle that is equidistant to them. Great circles through the two poles are called lines (or meridians) of longitude, and the line connecting the two poles is called the axis of rotation. Circles on the sphere that are parallel to the equator are lines of latitude.
    a. North pole
    b. Minimal surface
    c. Sphere
    d. Tangent line

20. For some curves there is a smallest number L that is an upper bound on the length of any polygonal approximation. If such a number exists, then the curve is said to be rectifiable and the curve is defined to have _____ L.

    Let C be a curve in Euclidean (or, generally, a metric) space X = R^n, so C is the image of a continuous function f : [a, b] → X of the interval [a, b] into X.

    a. Integration by parametric derivatives
    b. Arc length
    c. Order of integration
    d. Integrand

Chapter 2. Differential Calculus of Functions of Several Variables

21. In geometry, the _____ (or simply the tangent) to a curve at a given point is the straight line that 'just touches' the curve at that point (in the sense explained more precisely below.) As it passes through the point of tangency, the _____ is 'going in the same direction' as the curve, and in this sense it is the best straight-line approximation to the curve at that point. The same definition applies to space curves and curves in n-dimensional Euclidean space.
   a. North pole
   b. Tangent line
   c. Lie derivative
   d. Minimal surface

22. In physics, _____ is defined as the rate of change of position. it is vector physical quantity; both speed and direction are required to define it. In the SI (metric) system, it is measured in meters per second: (m/s) or ms^{-1}.
   a. Velocity
   b. 15 theorem
   c. BDDC
   d. BIBO stability

23. _____ is the long dimension of any object. The _____ of a thing is the distance between its ends, its linear extent as measured from end to end. This may be distinguished from height, which is vertical extent, and width or breadth, which are the distance from side to side, measuring across the object at right angles to the _____.
   a. BIBO stability
   b. Length
   c. 15 theorem
   d. BDDC

24. In vector calculus, _____ is a vector differential operator represented by the nabla symbol: ∇.

   _____ is a mathematical tool serving primarily as a convention for mathematical notation; it makes many equations easier to comprehend, write, and remember. Depending on the way _____ is applied, it can describe the gradient (slope), divergence (degree to which something converges or diverges) or curl (rotational motion at points in a fluid.)

   a. Del
   b. Triple product
   c. Divergence Theorem
   d. Green's theorem

25. In vector calculus, the _____ of a scalar field is a vector field which points in the direction of the greatest rate of increase of the scalar field, and whose magnitude is the greatest rate of change.

   A generalization of the _____ for functions on a Euclidean space which have values in another Euclidean space is the Jacobian. A further generalization for a function from one Banach space to another is the Fréchet derivative.

   a. Symmetric derivative
   b. Gradient
   c. Lin-Tsien equation
   d. Smooth function

26. In physics, and more specifically kinematics, _____ is the change in velocity over time. Because velocity is a vector, it can change in two ways: a change in magnitude and/or a change in direction. In one dimension, _____ is the rate at which something speeds up or slows down.
   a. ACTRAN
   b. ALGOR
   c. Acceleration
   d. AUSM

Chapter 2. Differential Calculus of Functions of Several Variables

27. In mathematics, _____ refers to any of a number of loosely related concepts in different areas of geometry. Intuitively, _____ is the amount by which a geometric object deviates from being flat, or straight in the case of a line, but this is defined in different ways depending on the context. There is a key distinction between extrinsic _____, which is defined for objects embedded in another space (usually a Euclidean space) in a way that relates to the radius of _____ of circles that touch the object, and intrinsic _____, which is defined at each point in a differential manifold.
   a. Minimal surface
   b. Sphere
   c. Lie derivative
   d. Curvature

28. In mathematics, the _____ of a power series is a non-negative quantity, either a real number or ∞, that represents a domain (within the radius) in which the series will converge. Within the _____, a power series converges absolutely and uniformly on compacta as well. If the series converges, it is the Taylor series of the analytic function to which it converges inside its _____.
   a. Blaschke product
   b. Branch point
   c. Holomorphically separable
   d. Radius of convergence

29. In mathematics, the _____ of a multivariate differentiable function along a given vector V at a given point P intuitively represents the instantaneous rate of change of the function, moving through P, in the direction of V. It therefore generalizes the notion of a partial derivative, in which the direction is always taken parallel to one of the coordinate axes.

   The _____ is a special case of the Gâteaux derivative.

   The _____ of a scalar function $f(\vec{x}) = f(x_1, x_2, \ldots, x_n)$ along a vector $\vec{v} = (v_1, \ldots, v_n)$ is the function defined by the limit

   $$\nabla_{\vec{v}} f(\vec{x}) = \lim_{h \to 0} \frac{f(\vec{x} + h\vec{v}) - f(\vec{x})}{h}.$$

   Sometimes authors write D_v instead of ∇_v.

   a. Symmetrically continuous
   b. Linearity of differentiation
   c. Directional derivative
   d. Differentiation of trigonometric functions

30. Let f be a differentiable function, and let f'(x) be its derivative. The derivative of f'(x) (if it has one) is written f''(x) and is called the _____ of f. Similarly, the derivative of a _____, if it exists, is written f'''(x) and is called the third derivative of f.
   a. Vertical asymptote
   b. Slant asymptote
   c. Stationary phase approximation
   d. Second derivative

31. In differential geometry there are a number of second-order, linear, elliptic differential operators bearing the name _____

   The connection _____ is a differential operator acting on the various tensor bundles of a manifold, defined in terms of a Riemmanian- or pseudo-Riemannian metric.

a. Dirac operator
b. Semi-elliptic operator
c. Laplacian
d. Peetre theorem

32. In mathematics, the _____ is a fourth-order partial differential equation which arises in areas of continuum mechanics, including linear elasticity theory and the solution of Stokes flows. It is written as

$$\nabla^4 \varphi = 0$$

where ∇^4 is the fourth power of the del operator and the square of the laplacian operator, and it is known as the biharmonic operator or the bilaplacian operator.

For example, in three dimensional cartesian coordinates the _____ has the form

$$\frac{\partial^4 \varphi}{\partial x^4} + \frac{\partial^4 \varphi}{\partial y^4} + \frac{\partial^4 \varphi}{\partial z^4} + 2\frac{\partial^4 \varphi}{\partial x^2 \partial y^2} + 2\frac{\partial^4 \varphi}{\partial y^2 \partial z^2} + 2\frac{\partial^4 \varphi}{\partial x^2 \partial z^2} = 0.$$

As another example, in n-dimensional Euclidean space,

$$\nabla^4 \left(\frac{1}{r}\right) = \frac{3(15 - 8n + n^2)}{r^5}$$

where

$$r = \sqrt{x_1^2 + x_2^2 + \cdots + x_n^2}.$$

which, for n=3 only, becomes the _____.

a. BDDC
b. Biharmonic equation
c. Hopf maximum principle
d. 15 theorem

33. In acoustics and telecommunication, a _____ of a wave is a component frequency of the signal that is an integer multiple of the fundamental frequency. For example, if the fundamental frequency is f, the harmonics have frequencies f, 2f, 3f, 4f, etc. The harmonics have the property that they are all periodic at the fundamental frequency, therefore the sum of harmonics is also periodic at that frequency.

a. 15 theorem
b. BIBO stability
c. Harmonic
d. BDDC

34. In mathematics, mathematical physics and the theory of stochastic processes, a _____ is a twice continuously differentiable function f : U → R (where U is an open subset of R^n) which satisfies Laplace's equation, i.e.

$$\frac{\partial^2 f}{\partial x_1^2} + \frac{\partial^2 f}{\partial x_2^2} + \cdots + \frac{\partial^2 f}{\partial x_n^2} = 0$$

everywhere on U. This is also often written as

$$\nabla^2 f = 0 \quad \text{or} \quad \Delta f = 0.$$

There also exists a seemingly weaker definition that is equivalent. Indeed a function is harmonic if and only if it is weakly harmonic.

Harmonic functions can be defined on an arbitrary Riemannian manifold, using the Laplace-de Rham operator Δ.

a. Kelvin transform
c. Maximum principle
b. Pluriharmonic function
d. Harmonic function

35. In geometry, for a finite planar surface of scalar area S, the vector area

S

is defined as a vector whose magnitude is S and whose direction is perpendicular to the plane, as determined by the right hand rule on the rim (moving one's right hand counterclockwise around the rim, when the palm of the hand is 'touching' the surface, and the straight thumb indicate the direction.)

$$\mathbf{S} = \hat{\mathbf{n}} S$$

This can only be defined for flat surfaces, or for regions of curved surfaces which are sufficiently small that they can be considered flat.

The concept of an _____ simplifies the equation for determining the flux through the surface.

a. ACTRAN
c. ALGOR
b. Orthogonal trajectories
d. Area vector

36. A _____ is a mathematical equation for an unknown function of one or several variables that relates the values of the function itself and of its derivatives of various orders. they play a prominent role in engineering, physics, economics and other disciplines.

A simplified real world example of a _____ is modeling the acceleration of a ball falling through the air (considering only gravity and air resistance.)

Chapter 2. Differential Calculus of Functions of Several Variables 15

a. Caloric polynomial
b. Structural stability
c. Phase line
d. Differential equation

37. In mathematics, in the field of differential equations, a _____ is a differential equation together with a set of additional restraints, called the boundary conditions. A solution to a _____ is a solution to the differential equation which also satisfies the boundary conditions.

Boundary value problems arise in several branches of physics as any physical differential equation will have them.

a. Spectral theory of ordinary differential equations
b. Variation of parameters
c. Mathieu functions
d. Boundary value problem

38. In mathematics, a _____ (or critical number) is a point on the domain of a function where:

- one dimension: the derivative (or slope of the line when visualized) is equal to zero or a point where the function ceases to be differentiable.
- in general: there are two distinct concepts: either the derivative (Jacobian) vanishes, or it is not of full rank (or, in either case, the function is not differentiable); these agree in one dimension.

Note that in one dimension, a critical value or critical number x of function f is the domain element at which the derivative is zero or undefined, whereas the associated ordered pair (x, y) is the _____. In higher dimensions a critical value is in the range whereas a _____ is in the domain.

There are two situations in which a point becomes a _____ of a function of one variable. The first of which is that the value of the first derivative is equal to zero.

a. Multivariable calculus
b. Total derivative
c. Differentiation operator
d. Critical point

39. Just as the definite integral of a positive function of one variable represents the area of the region between the graph of the function and the x-axis, the _____ of a positive function of two variables represents the volume of the region between the surface defined by the function (on the three dimensional Cartesian plane where z = f(x,y)) and the plane which contains its domain. (Note that the same volume can be obtained via the triple integral -- the integral of a function in three variables -- of the constant function f(x, y, z) = 1 over the above-mentioned region between the surface and the plane.) If there are more variables, a multiple integral will yield hypervolumes of multi-dimensional functions.

a. Constant of integration
b. Trigonometric substitution
c. Risch algorithm
d. Double integral

40. In differential calculus, an inflection point, or _____ (or inflexion) is a point on a curve at which the curvature changes sign. The curve changes from being concave upwards (positive curvature) to concave downwards (negative curvature), or vice versa. If one imagines driving a vehicle along the curve, it is a point at which the steering-wheel is momentarily 'straight', being turned from left to right or vice versa.

a. Derivative of a constant
b. Lin-Tsien equation
c. Logarithmic derivative
d. Point of inflection

Chapter 2. Differential Calculus of Functions of Several Variables

41. In mathematics, _____ and minima, known collectively as extrema, are the largest value (maximum) or smallest value (minimum), that a function takes in a point either within a given neighbourhood (local extremum) or on the function domain in its entirety (global extremum.)

Throughout, a point refers to an input (x), while a value refers to an output (y): one distinguishing between the maximum value and the point (or points) at which it occurs.

A real-valued function f defined on the real line is said to have a local maximum point at the point x^*, if there exists some $\varepsilon > 0$, such that $f(x^*) \geq f(x)$ when $|x - x^*| < \varepsilon$.

    a. Leibniz formula   b. Racetrack principle
    c. Related rates   d. Maxima

42. Integration is an important concept in mathematics, specifically in the field of calculus and, more broadly, mathematical analysis. Given a function f of a real variable x and an interval [a, b] of the real line, the _____

$$\int_a^b f(x)\, dx ,$$

is defined informally to be the net signed area of the region in the xy-plane bounded by the graph of f, the x-axis, and the vertical lines x = a and x = b.

The term '_____' may also refer to the notion of antiderivative, a function F whose derivative is the given function f.

    a. Integrand   b. Indefinite integral
    c. Integral test for convergence   d. Integral

43. In mathematics, a series (or sometimes also an integral) is said to converge absolutely if the sum (or integral) of the absolute value of the summand or integrand is finite.

More precisely, a real or complex-valued series $\sum_{n=0}^{\infty} a_n$ is said to converge absolutely if $\sum_{n=0}^{\infty} |a_n| < \infty$.

_____ is vitally important to the study of infinite series because on the one hand, it is strong enough that such series retain certain basic properties of finite sums -- the most important ones being rearrangement of the terms and convergence of products of two infinite series -- that are unfortunately not possessed by all convergent series. On the other hand _____ is weak enough to occur very often in practice.

    a. Absolute convergence   b. ACTRAN
    c. Eisenstein series   d. Alternating series test

Chapter 2. Differential Calculus of Functions of Several Variables

44. In a totally ordered set all elements are mutually comparable, so such a set can have at most one minimal element and at most one maximal element. Then, due to mutual comparability, the minimal element will also be the least element and the maximal element will also be the greatest element. Thus in a totally ordered set we can simply use the terms minimum and _____.

a. Maximum
b. Nth term
c. Leibniz rule
d. Racetrack principle

45. In a totally ordered set all elements are mutually comparable, so such a set can have at most one minimal element and at most one maximal element. Then, due to mutual comparability, the minimal element will also be the least element and the maximal element will also be the greatest element. Thus in a totally ordered set we can simply use the terms _____ and maximum.

a. Maximum
b. Ghosts of departed quantities
c. Minimum
d. Nth term

46. In mathematical optimization, the method of Lagrange multipliers provides a strategy for finding the maximum/minimum of a function subject to constraints.

For example, consider the optimization problem

$$\text{maximize } f(x, y)$$
$$\text{subject to } g(x, y) = c.$$

We introduce a new variable (λ) called a _____, and study the Lagrange function defined by

$$\Lambda(x, y, \lambda) = f(x, y) - \lambda\big(g(x, y) - c\big).$$

If (x,y) is a maximum for the original constrained problem, then there exists a λ such that (x,y,λ) is a stationary point for the Lagrange function (stationary points are those points where the partial derivatives of Λ are zero.) However, not all stationary points yield a solution of the original problem.

a. BIBO stability
b. 15 theorem
c. BDDC
d. Lagrange multiplier

47. The method of _____ or ordinary _____ is used to solve overdetermined systems. _____ is often applied in statistical contexts, particularly regression analysis.

_____ can be interpreted as a method of fitting data. The best fit in the _____ sense is that instance of the model for which the sum of squared residuals has its least value, a residual being the difference between an observed value and the value given by the model.

a. BDDC
b. BIBO stability
c. 15 theorem
d. Least squares

Chapter 2. Differential Calculus of Functions of Several Variables

48. A _____ of a function of two variables is a curve along which the function has a constant value. In cartography, a _____ (often just called a 'contour') joins points of equal elevation (height) above a given level, such as mean sea level. A contour map is a map illustrated with contour lines, for example a topographic map, which thus shows valleys and hills, and the steepness of slopes.
   a. 15 theorem
   b. BIBO stability
   c. BDDC
   d. Contour line

49. In computer science and information science, _____ could also be a method or an algorithm. Again, an example will illustrate: There are systems of counting, as with Roman numerals, and various systems for filing papers, or catalogues, and various library systems, of which the Dewey Decimal _____ is an example. This still fits with the definition of components which are connected together (in this case in order to facilitate the flow of information.)
   a. BIBO stability
   b. 15 theorem
   c. System
   d. BDDC

50. In mathematics the infimum of a subset of some set is the greatest element, not necessarily in the subset, that is less than or equal to all elements of the subset. Consequently the term _____ is also commonly used. Infima of real numbers are a common special case that is especially important in analysis.
   a. 15 theorem
   b. BIBO stability
   c. BDDC
   d. Greatest lower bound

51. In mathematics, given a subset S of a partially ordered set T, the _____ (sup) of S, if it exists, is the least element of T that is greater than or equal to each element of S. Consequently, the _____ is also referred to as the least upper bound, lub or LUB. If the _____ exists, it may or may not belong to S.
   a. BDDC
   b. BIBO stability
   c. 15 theorem
   d. Supremum

52. In real analysis, the _____ is a fundamental result about convergence in a finite-dimensional Euclidean space R^n. The theorem states that each bounded sequence in R^n has a convergent subsequence. An equivalent formulation is that a subset of R^n is sequentially compact if and only if it is closed and bounded.
   a. Multiplicative calculus
   b. Piecewise linear function
   c. Bolzano-Weierstrass theorem
   d. 15 theorem

53. In mathematics, especially in order theory, an upper bound of a subset S of some partially ordered set (P, ≤) is an element of P which is greater than or equal to every element of S. The term _____ is defined dually as an element of P which is lesser than or equal to every element of S. A set with an upper bound is said to be bounded from above by that bound, a set with a _____ is said to be bounded from below by that bound.

A subset S of a partially ordered set P may fail to have any bounds or may have many different upper and lower bounds. By transitivity, any element greater than or equal to an upper bound of S is again an upper bound of S, and any element lesser than or equal to any _____ of S is again a _____ of S. This leads to the consideration of least upper bounds: (or suprema) and greatest lower bounds (or infima.)

   a. 15 theorem
   b. Lower bound
   c. BIBO stability
   d. BDDC

54. In mathematics, especially in order theory, an _____ of a subset S of some partially ordered set (P, >≤) is an element of P which is greater than or equal to every element of S. The term lower bound is defined dually as an element of P which is lesser than or equal to every element of S. A set with an _____ is said to be bounded from above by that bound, a set with a lower bound is said to be bounded from below by that bound.

A subset S of a partially ordered set P may fail to have any bounds or may have many different upper and lower bounds. By transitivity, any element greater than or equal to an _____ of S is again an _____ of S, and any element lesser than or equal to any lower bound of S is again a lower bound of S. This leads to the consideration of least upper bounds: (or suprema) and greatest lower bounds (or infima.)

a. ALGOR
b. Upper bound
c. ACTRAN
d. AUSM

Chapter 3. Vector Differential Calculus

1. In vector calculus, the _____ is an operator that measures the magnitude of a vector field's source or sink at a given point; the _____ of a vector field is a (signed) scalar. For example, consider air as it is heated or cooled. The relevant vector field for this example is the velocity of the moving air at a point.
   - a. Green's theorem
   - b. Triple product
   - c. Divergence
   - d. Gradient theorem

2. In elementary mathematics, physics, and engineering, a _____ is a geometric object that has both a magnitude (or length), direction and sense, (i.e., orientation along the given direction.) A _____ is frequently represented by a line segment with a definite direction, or graphically as an arrow, connecting an initial point A with a terminal point B, and denoted by

   $\overrightarrow{\times}$

   The magnitude of the _____ is the length of the segment and the direction characterizes the displacement of B relative to A: how much one should move the point A to 'carry' it to the point B.

   Many algebraic operations on real numbers have close analogues for vectors.

   - a. Vector
   - b. 15 theorem
   - c. BDDC
   - d. Linear partial differential operator

3. Integration is an important concept in mathematics, specifically in the field of calculus and, more broadly, mathematical analysis. Given a function f of a real variable x and an interval [a, b] of the real line, the _____

   $$\int_a^b f(x)\, dx,$$

   is defined informally to be the net signed area of the region in the xy-plane bounded by the graph of f, the x-axis, and the vertical lines x = a and x = b.

   The term '_____' may also refer to the notion of antiderivative, a function F whose derivative is the given function f.

   - a. Integrand
   - b. Integral test for convergence
   - c. Indefinite integral
   - d. Integral

4. In mathematics, a _____ is an ordered list of objects (or events). Like a set, it contains members (also called elements or terms), and the number of terms (possibly infinite) is called the length of the _____. Unlike a set, order matters, and the exact same elements can appear multiple times at different positions in the _____.
   - a. Slope
   - b. Y-intercept
   - c. 15 theorem
   - d. Sequence

5. In mathematics a _____ is a construction in vector calculus which associates a vector to every point in a (locally) Euclidean space.

Chapter 3. Vector Differential Calculus

Vector fields are often used in physics to model, for example, the speed and direction of a moving fluid throughout space, or the strength and direction of some force, such as the magnetic or gravitational force, as it changes from point to point.

In the rigorous mathematical treatment, (tangent) vector fields are defined on manifolds as sections of a manifold's tangent bundle.

a. Vector field
b. 15 theorem
c. BDDC
d. BIBO stability

6. In vector calculus, _____ is a vector differential operator represented by the nabla symbol: ∇.

_____ is a mathematical tool serving primarily as a convention for mathematical notation; it makes many equations easier to comprehend, write, and remember. Depending on the way _____ is applied, it can describe the gradient (slope), divergence (degree to which something converges or diverges) or curl (rotational motion at points in a fluid.)

a. Triple product
b. Divergence Theorem
c. Green's theorem
d. Del

7. In mathematics, the _____ of a multivariate differentiable function along a given vector V at a given point P intuitively represents the instantaneous rate of change of the function, moving through P, in the direction of V. It therefore generalizes the notion of a partial derivative, in which the direction is always taken parallel to one of the coordinate axes.

The _____ is a special case of the Gâteaux derivative.

The _____ of a scalar function $f(\vec{x}) = f(x_1, x_2, \ldots, x_n)$ along a vector $\vec{v} = (v_1, \ldots, v_n)$ is the function defined by the limit

$$\nabla_{\vec{v}} f(\vec{x}) = \lim_{h \to 0} \frac{f(\vec{x} + h\vec{v}) - f(\vec{x})}{h}.$$

Sometimes authors write D_v instead of ∇v.

a. Directional derivative
b. Linearity of differentiation
c. Differentiation of trigonometric functions
d. Symmetrically continuous

8. In vector calculus, the _____ of a scalar field is a vector field which points in the direction of the greatest rate of increase of the scalar field, and whose magnitude is the greatest rate of change.

A generalization of the _____ for functions on a Euclidean space which have values in another Euclidean space is the Jacobian. A further generalization for a function from one Banach space to another is the Fréchet derivative.

a. Smooth function
c. Symmetric derivative
b. Lin-Tsien equation
d. Gradient

9. In calculus, a branch of mathematics, the _____ is a measurement of how a function changes when its input changes. Loosely speaking, a _____ can be thought of as how much a quantity is changing at some given point. For example, the _____ of the position (or distance) of a vehicle with respect to time is the instantaneous velocity (respectively, instantaneous speed) at which the vehicle is traveling.

The process of finding a _____ is called differentiation. The fundamental theorem of calculus states that differentiation is the reverse process to integration.

a. Bounded function
c. Semi-differentiability
b. Stationary phase approximation
d. Derivative

10. In mathematics, the _____ is the square matrix of second-order partial derivatives of a function; that is, it describes the local curvature of a function of many variables. The _____ was developed in the 19th century by the German mathematician Ludwig Otto Hesse and later named after him. Hesse himself had used the term 'functional determinants'.

a. Differentiation operator
c. Surface integral
b. Multivariable calculus
d. Hessian matrix

11. A _____ is a differential equation that describes the conservative transport of some kind of quantity. Since mass, energy, momentum, and other natural quantities are conserved, a vast variety of physics may be described with continuity equations.

All the examples of continuity equations below express the same idea.

a. 15 theorem
c. Continuity equation
b. BIBO stability
d. BDDC

12. The _____ of a material is defined as its mass per unit volume. The symbol of _____ is ρ '>rho.)

Mathematically:

$$d = \frac{m}{V}$$

where:

    d is the _____,
    m is the mass,
    V is the volume.

a. BIBO stability
b. Density
c. 15 theorem
d. BDDC

13. In vector calculus a conservative vector field is a vector field which is the gradient of a scalar potential. There are two closely related concepts: path independence and _____ vector fields. Every conservative vector field has zero curl (and is thus _____), and every conservative vector field has the path independence property.
   a. AUSM
   b. ACTRAN
   c. Irrotational
   d. ALGOR

14. In differential geometry there are a number of second-order, linear, elliptic differential operators bearing the name _____

The connection _____ is a differential operator acting on the various tensor bundles of a manifold, defined in terms of a Riemmanian- or pseudo-Riemannian metric.

   a. Laplacian
   b. Peetre theorem
   c. Dirac operator
   d. Semi-elliptic operator

15. In vector calculus a _____ vector field (also known as an incompressible vector field) is a vector field v with divergence zero:

$$\nabla \cdot \mathbf{v} = 0.$$

The fundamental theorem of vector calculus states that any vector field can be expressed as the sum of a conservative vector field and a _____ field. The condition of zero divergence is satisfied whenever a vector field v has only a vector potential component, because the definition of the vector potential A as:

$$\mathbf{v} = \nabla \times \mathbf{A}$$

automatically results in the identity (as can be shown, for example, using Cartesian coordinates):

$$\nabla \cdot \mathbf{v} = \nabla \cdot (\nabla \times \mathbf{A}) = 0.$$

The converse also holds: for any _____ v there exists a vector potential A such that $\mathbf{v} = \nabla \times \mathbf{A}$.

The divergence theorem, gives the equivalent integral definition of a _____ field; namely that for any closed surface S, the net total flux through the surface must be zero:

$$\iint_S \mathbf{v} \cdot d\mathbf{s} = 0$$

where $d\mathbf{s}$ is the outward normal to each surface element.

a. Solenoidal
b. Principal part
c. Bloch space
d. Trigonometric series

16. In acoustics and telecommunication, a _____ of a wave is a component frequency of the signal that is an integer multiple of the fundamental frequency. For example, if the fundamental frequency is f, the harmonics have frequencies f, 2f, 3f, 4f, etc. The harmonics have the property that they are all periodic at the fundamental frequency, therefore the sum of harmonics is also periodic at that frequency.
   a. BIBO stability
   b. BDDC
   c. 15 theorem
   d. Harmonic

17. In mathematics, mathematical physics and the theory of stochastic processes, a _____ is a twice continuously differentiable function f : U → R (where U is an open subset of R^n) which satisfies Laplace's equation, i.e.

$$\frac{\partial^2 f}{\partial x_1^2} + \frac{\partial^2 f}{\partial x_2^2} + \cdots + \frac{\partial^2 f}{\partial x_n^2} = 0$$

everywhere on U. This is also often written as

$$\nabla^2 f = 0 \quad \text{or} \quad \Delta f = 0.$$

There also exists a seemingly weaker definition that is equivalent. Indeed a function is harmonic if and only if it is weakly harmonic.

Harmonic functions can be defined on an arbitrary Riemannian manifold, using the Laplace-de Rham operator Δ.

   a. Maximum principle
   b. Pluriharmonic function
   c. Kelvin transform
   d. Harmonic function

18. In physics, _____ is defined as the rate of change of position. it is vector physical quantity; both speed and direction are required to define it. In the SI (metric) system, it is measured in meters per second: (m/s) or ms^{-1}.
   a. BIBO stability
   b. BDDC
   c. 15 theorem
   d. Velocity

19. In mathematics and its applications, a _____ system is a system for assigning an n-tuple of numbers or scalars to each point in an n-dimensional space. This concept is part of the theory of manifolds. 'Scalars' in many cases means real numbers, but, depending on context, can mean complex numbers or elements of some other commutative ring.
   a. Cylindrical coordinate system
   b. Coordinate
   c. 15 theorem
   d. Spherical coordinate system

20. For some curves there is a smallest number L that is an upper bound on the length of any polygonal approximation. If such a number exists, then the curve is said to be rectifiable and the curve is defined to have _____ L.

Let C be a curve in Euclidean (or, generally, a metric) space X = R^n, so C is the image of a continuous function f : [a, b] → X of the interval [a, b] into X.

a. Integrand
b. Arc length
c. Integration by parametric derivatives
d. Order of integration

21. In mathematics, two vectors are _____ if they are perpendicular, i.e., they form a right angle. For example, a subway and the street above, although they do not physically intersect, are _____ if they cross at a right angle.
   a. ACTRAN
   b. Orthogonal
   c. AUSM
   d. ALGOR

22. _____ is the long dimension of any object. The _____ of a thing is the distance between its ends, its linear extent as measured from end to end. This may be distinguished from height, which is vertical extent, and width or breadth, which are the distance from side to side, measuring across the object at right angles to the _____.
   a. Length
   b. 15 theorem
   c. BIBO stability
   d. BDDC

23. If a particular point on a sphere is (arbitrarily) designated as its _____, then the corresponding antipodal point is called the south pole and the equator is the great circle that is equidistant to them. Great circles through the two poles are called lines (or meridians) of longitude, and the line connecting the two poles is called the axis of rotation. Circles on the sphere that are parallel to the equator are lines of latitude.
   a. North pole
   b. Minimal surface
   c. Sphere
   d. Tangent line

24. A _____ is one of the most curvilinear basic geometric shapes:It has two faces, zero vertices, and zero edges. The surface formed by the points at a fixed distance from a given straight line, the axis of the _____. The solid enclosed by this surface and by two planes perpendicular to the axis is also called a _____.
   a. BDDC
   b. 15 theorem
   c. Cylinder
   d. Right circular cylinder

25. In geometry, for a finite planar surface of scalar area S, the vector area

$$\mathbf{S}$$

is defined as a vector whose magnitude is S and whose direction is perpendicular to the plane, as determined by the right hand rule on the rim (moving one's right hand counterclockwise around the rim, when the palm of the hand is 'touching' the surface, and the straight thumb indicate the direction.)

$$\mathbf{S} = \hat{\mathbf{n}} S$$

This can only be defined for flat surfaces, or for regions of curved surfaces which are sufficiently small that they can be considered flat.

The concept of an _____ simplifies the equation for determining the flux through the surface.

   a. ALGOR
   b. ACTRAN
   c. Area vector
   d. Orthogonal trajectories

26. In mathematics, _____ refers to any of a number of loosely related concepts in different areas of geometry. Intuitively, _____ is the amount by which a geometric object deviates from being flat, or straight in the case of a line, but this is defined in different ways depending on the context. There is a key distinction between extrinsic _____, which is defined for objects embedded in another space (usually a Euclidean space) in a way that relates to the radius of _____ of circles that touch the object, and intrinsic _____, which is defined at each point in a differential manifold.
   a. Lie derivative
   b. Curvature
   c. Minimal surface
   d. Sphere

Chapter 4. Integral Calculus of Functions of Several Variables

1. In the branch of mathematics known as real analysis, the _____, created by Bernhard Riemann, was the first rigorous definition of the integral of a function on an interval. While the _____ is unsuitable for many theoretical purposes, it is one of the easiest integrals to define. Some of these technical deficiencies can be remedied by the Riemann-Stieltjes integral, and most of them disappear in the Lebesgue integral.
   a. Regulated integral
   b. Skorokhod integral
   c. Riemann integral
   d. Lebesgue integration

2. Integration is an important concept in mathematics, specifically in the field of calculus and, more broadly, mathematical analysis. Given a function f of a real variable x and an interval [a, b] of the real line, the _____

$$\int_a^b f(x)\,dx,$$

is defined informally to be the net signed area of the region in the xy-plane bounded by the graph of f, the x-axis, and the vertical lines x = a and x = b.

The term '_____' may also refer to the notion of antiderivative, a function F whose derivative is the given function f.

   a. Integral test for convergence
   b. Integrand
   c. Indefinite integral
   d. Integral

3. In calculus, an antiderivative, primitive or _____ of a function f is a function F whose derivative is equal to f, i.e., F ' = f. The process of solving for antiderivatives is antidifferentiation (or indefinite integration.) Antiderivatives are related to definite integrals through the fundamental theorem of calculus: the definite integral of a function over an interval is equal to the difference between the values of an antiderivative evaluated at the endpoints of the interval.
   a. Integration by parts operator
   b. Integral test for convergence
   c. Arc length
   d. Indefinite integral

4. In infinitesimal calculus, a _____ is traditionally an infinitesimally small change in a variable. For example, if x is a variable, then a change in the value of x is often denoted Δx (or δx when this change is considered to be small.) The _____ dx represents such a change, but is infinitely small.
   a. Local maximum
   b. The Method of Mechanical Theorems
   c. Differential
   d. Dirichlet integral

5. In mathematics and statistics, the _____ of a list of numbers is the sum of all of the list divided by the number of items in the list. If the list is a statistical population, then the mean of that population is called a population mean. If the list is a statistical sample, we call the resulting statistic a sample mean.
   a. AUSM
   b. ALGOR
   c. ACTRAN
   d. Arithmetic mean

6. In calculus, and more generally in mathematical analysis, _____ is a rule that transforms the integral of products of functions into other, hopefully simpler, integrals. The rule arises from the product rule of differentiation.

If u = f(x), v = g(x), and the differentials du = f '(x) dx and dv = g'(x) dx; then in its simplest form the product rule is:

$$\int u\,dv = uv - \int v\,du.$$

Suppose f(x) and g(x) are two continuously differentiable functions.

a. Arc length
b. Integrand
c. Integration by parametric derivatives
d. Integration by parts

7. In probability theory and statistics, the _____ (or expectation value or mean and for continuous random variables with a density function it is the probability density -weighted integral of the possible values.

The term '_____' can be misleading.

a. ACTRAN
b. ALGOR
c. AUSM
d. Expected value

8. A _____ of a function of two variables is a curve along which the function has a constant value. In cartography, a _____ (often just called a 'contour') joins points of equal elevation (height) above a given level, such as mean sea level. A contour map is a map illustrated with contour lines, for example a topographic map, which thus shows valleys and hills, and the steepness of slopes.

a. 15 theorem
b. BDDC
c. BIBO stability
d. Contour line

9. In calculus, an _____ is the limit of a definite integral as an endpoint of the interval of integration approaches either a specified real number or ∞ or −∞ or, in some cases, as both endpoints approach limits.

Specifically, an _____ is a limit of the form

$$\lim_{b \to \infty} \int_a^b f(x)\,dx, \qquad \lim_{a \to -\infty} \int_a^b f(x)\,dx,$$

or of the form

$$\lim_{c \to b^-} \int_a^c f(x)\,dx, \qquad \lim_{c \to a^+} \int_c^b f(x)\,dx,$$

in which one takes a limit in one or the other (or sometimes both) endpoints . Improper integrals may also occur at an interior point of the domain of integration, or at multiple such points.

Chapter 4. Integral Calculus of Functions of Several Variables

a. Improper integral
c. ACTRAN
b. AUSM
d. ALGOR

10. In mathematics, the _____ is a way to approximately calculate the definite integral

$$\int_a^b f(x)\,dx.$$

The _____ works by approximating the region under the graph of the function f by a trapezoid and calculating its area. It follows that

$$\int_a^b f(x)\,dx \approx (b-a)\frac{f(a)+f(b)}{2}.$$

To calculate this integral more accurately, one first splits the interval of integration [a,b] into n smaller subintervals, and then applies the _____ on each of them. One obtains the composite _____:

$$\int_a^b f(x)\,dx \approx \frac{b-a}{n}\left[\frac{f(a)+f(b)}{2} + \sum_{k=1}^{n-1} f\left(a+k\frac{b-a}{n}\right)\right].$$

This can alternatively be written as:

$$\int_a^b f(x)\,dx \approx \frac{b-a}{2n}\left(f(x_0)+2f(x_1)+2f(x_2)+\cdots+2f(x_{n-1})+f(x_n)\right)$$

where

$$x_k = a + k\frac{b-a}{n}, \text{ for } k=0,1,\ldots,n$$

(one can also use a non-uniform grid.)

a. BIBO stability
c. 15 theorem
b. BDDC
d. Trapezoidal rule

11. In computer science and information science, _____ could also be a method or an algorithm. Again, an example will illustrate: There are systems of counting, as with Roman numerals, and various systems for filing papers, or catalogues, and various library systems, of which the Dewey Decimal _____ is an example. This still fits with the definition of components which are connected together (in this case in order to facilitate the flow of information.)

a. BDDC
c. 15 theorem
b. BIBO stability
d. System

Chapter 4. Integral Calculus of Functions of Several Variables

12. A _____ is a mathematical equation for an unknown function of one or several variables that relates the values of the function itself and of its derivatives of various orders. they play a prominent role in engineering, physics, economics and other disciplines.

A simplified real world example of a _____ is modeling the acceleration of a ball falling through the air (considering only gravity and air resistance.)

a. Caloric polynomial
b. Phase line
c. Structural stability
d. Differential equation

13. Just as the definite integral of a positive function of one variable represents the area of the region between the graph of the function and the x-axis, the _____ of a positive function of two variables represents the volume of the region between the surface defined by the function (on the three dimensional Cartesian plane where z = f(x,y)) and the plane which contains its domain. (Note that the same volume can be obtained via the triple integral -- the integral of a function in three variables -- of the constant function f(x, y, z) = 1 over the above-mentioned region between the surface and the plane.) If there are more variables, a multiple integral will yield hypervolumes of multi-dimensional functions.

a. Constant of integration
b. Risch algorithm
c. Double integral
d. Trigonometric substitution

14. The _____ of any solid, liquid, plasma, vacuum or theoretical object is how much three-dimensional space it occupies, often quantified numerically. One-dimensional figures (such as lines) and two-dimensional shapes (such as squares) are assigned zero _____ in the three-dimensional space. _____ is commonly presented in units such as mL or cm^3 (milliliters or cubic centimeters.)

a. Klein-Gordon equation
b. Dirac equation
c. Vector potential
d. Volume

15. The _____ of a system of particles is a specific point at which, for many purposes, the system's mass behaves as if it were concentrated. The _____ is a function only of the positions and masses of the particles that comprise the system. In the case of a rigid body, the position of its _____ is fixed in relation to the object (but not necessarily in contact with it.)

a. 15 theorem
b. Simple harmonic motion
c. Center of mass
d. Fundamental lemma in the calculus of variations

16. The concept of _____ in mathematics evolved from the concept of _____ in physics. The nth _____ of a real-valued function f(x) of a real variable about a value c is

$$\mu'_n = \int_{-\infty}^{\infty} (x - c)^n f(x)\, dx.$$

It is possible to define moments for random variables in a more general fashion than moments for real values. See Moments in metric spaces.

a. Poisson distribution
b. Moment
c. Median
d. Geometric mean

17. _____, also called mass _____ or the angular mass, (SI units kg m^2) is a measure of an object's resistance to changes in its rotation rate. It is the rotational analog of mass. That is, it is the inertia of a rigid rotating body with respect to its rotation.
   a. Moment of inertia
   b. Wave equation
   c. Dirac equation
   d. Klein-Gordon equation

18. In mathematics, the _____ is a two-dimensional coordinate system in which each point on a plane is determined by an angle and a distance. The _____ is especially useful in situations where the relationship between two points is most easily expressed in terms of angles and distance; in the more familiar Cartesian or rectangular coordinate system, such a relationship can only be found through trigonometric formulation.

As the coordinate system is two-dimensional, each point is determined by two polar coordinates: the radial coordinate and the angular coordinate.

   a. BDDC
   b. BIBO stability
   c. Polar coordinate system
   d. 15 theorem

19. In mathematics and its applications, a _____ system is a system for assigning an n-tuple of numbers or scalars to each point in an n-dimensional space. This concept is part of the theory of manifolds. 'Scalars' in many cases means real numbers, but, depending on context, can mean complex numbers or elements of some other commutative ring.
   a. 15 theorem
   b. Coordinate
   c. Cylindrical coordinate system
   d. Spherical coordinate system

20. The _____ of a material is defined as its mass per unit volume. The symbol of _____ is ρ '>rho.)

Mathematically:

$$d = \frac{m}{V}$$

where:

    d is the _____,
    m is the mass,
    V is the volume.

   a. 15 theorem
   b. Density
   c. BIBO stability
   d. BDDC

21. In mathematics, a _____ decomposes a periodic function into a sum of simple oscillating functions, namely sines and cosines (or complex exponentials.) The study of _____ is a branch of Fourier analysis. _____ were introduced by Joseph Fourier (1768-1830) for the purpose of solving the heat equation in a metal plate.
   a. BDDC
   b. BIBO stability
   c. 15 theorem
   d. Fourier series

Chapter 4. Integral Calculus of Functions of Several Variables

22. The _____ is a type of definite integral extended to functions of more than one real variable, for example, f(x, y) or f (x, y, z.)

Introduction

Just as the definite integral of a positive function of one variable represents the area of the region between the graph of the function and the x-axis, the double integral of a positive function of two variables represents the volume of the region between the surface defined by the function (on the three dimensional Cartesian plane where z = f(x,y)) and the plane which contains its domain. (Note that the same volume can be obtained via the triple integral -- the integral of a function in three variables -- of the constant function f(x, y, z) = 1 over the above-mentioned region between the surface and the plane.)

   a. Quadratic integral   b. Surface of revolution
   c. Multiple integral   d. Risch algorithm

23. In elementary mathematics, physics, and engineering, a _____ is a geometric object that has both a magnitude (or length), direction and sense, (i.e., orientation along the given direction.) A _____ is frequently represented by a line segment with a definite direction, or graphically as an arrow, connecting an initial point A with a terminal point B, and denoted by

The magnitude of the _____ is the length of the segment and the direction characterizes the displacement of B relative to A: how much one should move the point A to 'carry' it to the point B.

Many algebraic operations on real numbers have close analogues for vectors.

   a. BDDC   b. 15 theorem
   c. Linear partial differential operator   d. Vector

24. An _____ is a type of quadric surface that is a higher dimensional analogue of an ellipse. The equation of a standard axis-aligned _____ body in an xyz-Cartesian coordinate system is

$$\frac{x^2}{a^2} + \frac{y^2}{b^2} + \frac{z^2}{c^2} = 1$$

where a and b are the equatorial radii (along the x and y axes) and c is the polar radius (along the z-axis), all of which are fixed positive real numbers determining the shape of the _____.

More generally, a not-necessarily-axis-aligned _____ is defined by the equation

$$\mathbf{x}^T A \mathbf{x} = 1$$

where A is a symmetric positive definite matrix and x is a vector.

a. AUSM
b. ACTRAN
c. ALGOR
d. Ellipsoid

25. For some curves there is a smallest number L that is an upper bound on the length of any polygonal approximation. If such a number exists, then the curve is said to be rectifiable and the curve is defined to have _____ L.

Let C be a curve in Euclidean (or, generally, a metric) space X = R^n, so C is the image of a continuous function f : [a, b] → X of the interval [a, b] into X.

a. Integration by parametric derivatives
b. Integrand
c. Order of integration
d. Arc length

26. _____ is the long dimension of any object. The _____ of a thing is the distance between its ends, its linear extent as measured from end to end. This may be distinguished from height, which is vertical extent, and width or breadth, which are the distance from side to side, measuring across the object at right angles to the _____.

a. BIBO stability
b. BDDC
c. 15 theorem
d. Length

27. A _____ is a surface created by rotating a curve lying on some plane (the generatrix) around a straight line (the axis of rotation) that lies on the same plane.

Examples of surfaces generated by a straight line are the cylindrical and conical surfaces. A circle that is rotated about a (coplanar) axis through the center generates a sphere.

a. Surface of revolution
b. Riemann sum
c. Shell integration
d. Constant of integration

28. In mathematics, specifically in calculus and complex analysis, the _____ of a function f is defined by the formula

$$\frac{f'}{f}$$

where f ' is the derivative of f.

When f is a function f(x) of a real variable x, and takes real, strictly positive values, this is indeed the formula for (log f)', that is, the derivative of the natural logarithm of f, as follows directly from the chain rule.

Many properties of the real logarithm also apply to the _____, even when the function does not take values in the positive reals.

a. Lin-Tsien equation
b. Logarithmic derivative
c. Directional derivative
d. Point of inflection

29. In calculus, a branch of mathematics, the _____ is a measurement of how a function changes when its input changes. Loosely speaking, a _____ can be thought of as how much a quantity is changing at some given point. For example, the _____ of the position (or distance) of a vehicle with respect to time is the instantaneous velocity (respectively, instantaneous speed) at which the vehicle is traveling.

The process of finding a _____ is called differentiation. The fundamental theorem of calculus states that differentiation is the reverse process to integration.

 a. Bounded function   b. Semi-differentiability
 c. Stationary phase approximation   d. Derivative

30. In mathematics, the _____ is an operator in vector calculus that acts as the inverse to the negative Laplacian, on functions that are smooth and decay rapidly enough at infinity. In its general nature, it is a singular integral operator, defined by convolution with a function having a mathematical singularity at the origin, the Newtonian kernel G which is the fundamental solution of the Laplace equation.

Stating its property in another way, the _____ applied to a function f satisfies Poisson's equation with f as RHS.

 a. Newtonian potential   b. Harmonic function
 c. Kelvin transform   d. Hilbert transform

31. A _____ is a set of standard clothing worn by members of an organization while participating in that organization's activity. Modern uniforms are worn by armed forces and paramilitary organisations such as police, emergency services, security guards, in some workplaces and schools and by inmates in prisons. In some countries, some other officials also wear uniforms in their duties; such is the case of the Commissioned Corps of the United States Public Health Service or the French prefects.

 a. AUSM   b. Uniform
 c. ALGOR   d. ACTRAN

32. In mathematics, a function f is uniformly continuous if, roughly speaking, it is possible to guarantee that $f(x)$ and $f(y)$ be as close to each other as we please by requiring only that x and y are sufficiently close to each other; unlike ordinary continuity, the maximum distance between $f(x)$ and $f(y)$ cannot depend on x and y themselves. For instance, any isometry (distance-preserving map) between metric spaces is uniformly continuous.

_____, unlike continuity, is meaningless in an arbitrary topological space, since it relies on the ability to compare the sizes of neighbourhoods of distinct points of a space.

 a. AUSM   b. Uniform continuity
 c. ALGOR   d. ACTRAN

Chapter 5. Vector Integral Calculus

1. In mathematics, a _____ is an integral where the function to be integrated is evaluated along a curve. Various different line integrals are in use. A specific case of an integration along a closed curve in two dimensions or the complex plane is the contour integral.

   a. Picard theorem   b. Line integral
   c. Mittag-Leffler star   d. Radius of convergence

2. In elementary mathematics, physics, and engineering, a _____ is a geometric object that has both a magnitude (or length), direction and sense, (i.e., orientation along the given direction.) A _____ is frequently represented by a line segment with a definite direction, or graphically as an arrow, connecting an initial point A with a terminal point B, and denoted by

$\overrightarrow{\square}$

The magnitude of the _____ is the length of the segment and the direction characterizes the displacement of B relative to A: how much one should move the point A to 'carry' it to the point B.

Many algebraic operations on real numbers have close analogues for vectors.

   a. 15 theorem   b. BDDC
   c. Vector   d. Linear partial differential operator

3. Integration is an important concept in mathematics, specifically in the field of calculus and, more broadly, mathematical analysis. Given a function f of a real variable x and an interval [a, b] of the real line, the _____

$$\int_a^b f(x)\, dx,$$

is defined informally to be the net signed area of the region in the xy-plane bounded by the graph of f, the x-axis, and the vertical lines x = a and x = b.

The term '_____' may also refer to the notion of antiderivative, a function F whose derivative is the given function f.

   a. Integrand   b. Indefinite integral
   c. Integral   d. Integral test for convergence

4. A curve γ is said to be closed or a loop if $I = [a, b]$ and if $\gamma(a) = \gamma(b)$. A _____ is thus a continuous mapping of the circle S^1; a simple _____ is also called a Jordan curve or a Jordan arc. The Jordan curve theorem states that such curves divide the plane into an 'interior' and an 'exterior'.

   a. Kappa curve   b. Curve
   c. Bullet-nose curve   d. Closed curve

5. A _____ is a type of manifold that is locally similar enough to Euclidean space to allow one to do calculus Any manifold can be described by a collection of charts, also known as an atlas.

Chapter 5. Vector Integral Calculus

a. Sphere
b. Tangent line
c. Differentiable manifold
d. Minimal surface

6. _____ is how much exposed area an object has. It is expressed in square units. If an object has flat faces, its _____ can be calculated by adding together the areas of its faces.

a. Surface area
b. Lipschitz domain
c. Vector area
d. Plane curve

7. In geometry, for a finite planar surface of scalar area S, the vector area

$$\mathbf{S}$$

is defined as a vector whose magnitude is S and whose direction is perpendicular to the plane, as determined by the right hand rule on the rim (moving one's right hand counterclockwise around the rim, when the palm of the hand is 'touching' the surface, and the straight thumb indicate the direction.)

$$\mathbf{S} = \hat{\mathbf{n}} S$$

This can only be defined for flat surfaces, or for regions of curved surfaces which are sufficiently small that they can be considered flat.

The concept of an _____ simplifies the equation for determining the flux through the surface.

a. ALGOR
b. Orthogonal trajectories
c. ACTRAN
d. Area vector

8. In mathematics, a (topological) _____ is defined as follows: let I be an interval of real numbers (i.e. a non-empty connected subset of $\mathbb{R}$); then a _____ γ is a continuous mapping $\gamma : I \to X$, where X is a topological space. The _____ γ is said to be simple if it is injective, i.e. if for all x, y in I, we have $\gamma(x) = \gamma(y) \implies x = y$. If I is a closed bounded interval $[a, b]$, we also allow the possibility $\gamma(a) = \gamma(b)$ (this convention makes it possible to talk about closed simple _____.)

a. Curve
b. Prolate cycloid
c. Tractrix
d. Closed curve

9. In mathematics, a _____ is a function whose definition is dependent on the value of the independent variable. Mathematically, a real-valued function f of a real variable x is a relationship whose definition is given differently on disjoint subsets of its domain

The word piecewise is also used to describe any property of a _____ that holds for each piece but may not hold for the whole domain of the function.

a. Constant function
b. Range
c. Surjective
d. Piecewise-defined function

Chapter 5. Vector Integral Calculus

10. For some curves there is a smallest number L that is an upper bound on the length of any polygonal approximation. If such a number exists, then the curve is said to be rectifiable and the curve is defined to have _____ L.

Let C be a curve in Euclidean (or, generally, a metric) space $X = R^n$, so C is the image of a continuous function f : [a, b] → X of the interval [a, b] into X.

- a. Order of integration
- b. Integrand
- c. Integration by parametric derivatives
- d. Arc length

11. _____ is the long dimension of any object. The _____ of a thing is the distance between its ends, its linear extent as measured from end to end. This may be distinguished from height, which is vertical extent, and width or breadth, which are the distance from side to side, measuring across the object at right angles to the _____.
- a. Length
- b. BDDC
- c. BIBO stability
- d. 15 theorem

12. The _____ of an object is the extra energy which it possesses due to its motion. It is defined as the work needed to accelerate a body of a given mass from rest to its current velocity. Having gained this energy during its acceleration, the body maintains this _____ unless its speed changes.
- a. Law of Conservation of Energy
- b. 15 theorem
- c. BDDC
- d. Kinetic energy

13. In calculus, a branch of mathematics, the _____ is a measurement of how a function changes when its input changes. Loosely speaking, a _____ can be thought of as how much a quantity is changing at some given point. For example, the _____ of the position (or distance) of a vehicle with respect to time is the instantaneous velocity (respectively, instantaneous speed) at which the vehicle is traveling.

The process of finding a _____ is called differentiation. The fundamental theorem of calculus states that differentiation is the reverse process to integration.

- a. Semi-differentiability
- b. Derivative
- c. Bounded function
- d. Stationary phase approximation

14. In vector calculus, the _____ is an operator that measures the magnitude of a vector field's source or sink at a given point; the _____ of a vector field is a (signed) scalar. For example, consider air as it is heated or cooled. The relevant vector field for this example is the velocity of the moving air at a point.
- a. Green's theorem
- b. Gradient theorem
- c. Divergence
- d. Triple product

15. In mathematics, a _____ is an ordered list of objects (or events). Like a set, it contains members (also called elements or terms), and the number of terms (possibly infinite) is called the length of the _____. Unlike a set, order matters, and the exact same elements can appear multiple times at different positions in the _____.
- a. Y-intercept
- b. Slope
- c. 15 theorem
- d. Sequence

16. In mathematics a _____ is a construction in vector calculus which associates a vector to every point in a (locally) Euclidean space.

Chapter 5. Vector Integral Calculus

Vector fields are often used in physics to model, for example, the speed and direction of a moving fluid throughout space, or the strength and direction of some force, such as the magnetic or gravitational force, as it changes from point to point.

In the rigorous mathematical treatment, (tangent) vector fields are defined on manifolds as sections of a manifold's tangent bundle.

    a. BIBO stability
    b. Vector field
    c. 15 theorem
    d. BDDC

17. In vector calculus, the _____ of a scalar field is a vector field which points in the direction of the greatest rate of increase of the scalar field, and whose magnitude is the greatest rate of change.

A generalization of the _____ for functions on a Euclidean space which have values in another Euclidean space is the Jacobian. A further generalization for a function from one Banach space to another is the Fréchet derivative.

    a. Gradient
    b. Symmetric derivative
    c. Smooth function
    d. Lin-Tsien equation

18. A _____ of a function of two variables is a curve along which the function has a constant value. In cartography, a _____ (often just called a 'contour') joins points of equal elevation (height) above a given level, such as mean sea level. A contour map is a map illustrated with contour lines, for example a topographic map, which thus shows valleys and hills, and the steepness of slopes.

    a. Contour line
    b. BDDC
    c. BIBO stability
    d. 15 theorem

19. In calculus, an _____ is the limit of a definite integral as an endpoint of the interval of integration approaches either a specified real number or ∞ or −∞ or, in some cases, as both endpoints approach limits.

Specifically, an _____ is a limit of the form

$$\lim_{b \to \infty} \int_a^b f(x)\,dx, \qquad \lim_{a \to -\infty} \int_a^b f(x)\,dx,$$

or of the form

$$\lim_{c \to b^-} \int_a^c f(x)\,dx, \qquad \lim_{c \to a^+} \int_c^b f(x)\,dx,$$

in which one takes a limit in one or the other (or sometimes both) endpoints . Improper integrals may also occur at an interior point of the domain of integration, or at multiple such points.

Chapter 5. Vector Integral Calculus

a. AUSM
b. ALGOR
c. ACTRAN
d. Improper integral

20. In mathematics, the _____ of a closed curve in the plane around a given point is an integer representing the total number of times that curve travels counterclockwise around the point. The _____ depends on the orientation of the curve, and is negative if the curve travels around the point clockwise.

Winding numbers are fundamental objects of study in algebraic topology, and they play an important role in vector calculus, complex analysis, geometric topology, differential geometry, and physics.

a. BDDC
b. Winding number
c. BIBO stability
d. 15 theorem

21. A surface S in the Euclidean space R^3 is _____ if a two-dimensional figure (for example,) cannot be moved around the surface and back to where it started so that it looks like its own mirror image (.) Otherwise the surface is non-_____.

More precisely, and applicable to non-embedded surfaces, a surface is non-_____ if there is a continuous map f from the product of a 2-dimensional disk D and the unit interval [0,1] to the surface, $f : D \times [0, 1] \to S$ such that f(c,t) = f(d,t) only if c = d for every t in [0,1], and there exists a reflection map r such that f(d,0) = f(r(d),1) for every d in D.

a. ACTRAN
b. AUSM
c. ALGOR
d. Orientable

22. In mathematics, a _____ is a definite integral taken over a surface (which may be a curved set in space); it can be thought of as the double integral analog of the line integral. Given a surface, one may integrate over it scalar fields (that is, functions which return numbers as values), and vector fields (that is, functions which return vectors as values.)

Surface integrals have applications in physics, particularly with the classical theory of electromagnetism.

a. Differential operator
b. Contact
c. Symmetry of second derivatives
d. Surface integral

23. The _____ of a system of particles is a specific point at which, for many purposes, the system's mass behaves as if it were concentrated. The _____ is a function only of the positions and masses of the particles that comprise the system. In the case of a rigid body, the position of its _____ is fixed in relation to the object (but not necessarily in contact with it.)

a. Center of mass
b. Fundamental lemma in the calculus of variations
c. 15 theorem
d. Simple harmonic motion

24. The concept of _____ in mathematics evolved from the concept of _____ in physics. The nth _____ of a real-valued function f(x) of a real variable about a value c is

$$\mu'_n = \int_{-\infty}^{\infty} (x-c)^n f(x)\, dx.$$

It is possible to define moments for random variables in a more general fashion than moments for real values. See Moments in metric spaces.

a. Geometric mean
b. Moment
c. Median
d. Poisson distribution

25. _____, also called mass _____ or the angular mass, (SI units kg m^2) is a measure of an object's resistance to changes in its rotation rate. It is the rotational analog of mass. That is, it is the inertia of a rigid rotating body with respect to its rotation.

a. Dirac equation
b. Klein-Gordon equation
c. Wave equation
d. Moment of inertia

26. A _____ is a differential equation that describes the conservative transport of some kind of quantity. Since mass, energy, momentum, and other natural quantities are conserved, a vast variety of physics may be described with continuity equations.

All the examples of continuity equations below express the same idea.

a. Continuity equation
b. BIBO stability
c. 15 theorem
d. BDDC

27. In acoustics and telecommunication, a _____ of a wave is a component frequency of the signal that is an integer multiple of the fundamental frequency. For example, if the fundamental frequency is f, the harmonics have frequencies f, 2f, 3f, 4f, etc. The harmonics have the property that they are all periodic at the fundamental frequency, therefore the sum of harmonics is also periodic at that frequency.

a. Harmonic
b. 15 theorem
c. BDDC
d. BIBO stability

28. In mathematics, mathematical physics and the theory of stochastic processes, a _____ is a twice continuously differentiable function f : U → R (where U is an open subset of R^n) which satisfies Laplace's equation, i.e.

$$\frac{\partial^2 f}{\partial x_1^2} + \frac{\partial^2 f}{\partial x_2^2} + \cdots + \frac{\partial^2 f}{\partial x_n^2} = 0$$

everywhere on U. This is also often written as

$$\nabla^2 f = 0 \quad \text{or} \quad \Delta f = 0.$$

There also exists a seemingly weaker definition that is equivalent. Indeed a function is harmonic if and only if it is weakly harmonic.

Harmonic functions can be defined on an arbitrary Riemannian manifold, using the Laplace-de Rham operator Δ.

a. Maximum principle
b. Pluriharmonic function
c. Kelvin transform
d. Harmonic function

29. In vector calculus a conservative vector field is a vector field which is the gradient of a scalar potential. There are two closely related concepts: path independence and _____ vector fields. Every conservative vector field has zero curl (and is thus _____), and every conservative vector field has the path independence property.

a. ACTRAN
b. AUSM
c. Irrotational
d. ALGOR

30. In vector calculus a _____ vector field (also known as an incompressible vector field) is a vector field v with divergence zero:

$$\nabla \cdot \mathbf{v} = 0.$$

The fundamental theorem of vector calculus states that any vector field can be expressed as the sum of a conservative vector field and a _____ field. The condition of zero divergence is satisfied whenever a vector field v has only a vector potential component, because the definition of the vector potential A as:

$$\mathbf{v} = \nabla \times \mathbf{A}$$

automatically results in the identity (as can be shown, for example, using Cartesian coordinates):

$$\nabla \cdot \mathbf{v} = \nabla \cdot (\nabla \times \mathbf{A}) = 0.$$

The converse also holds: for any _____ v there exists a vector potential A such that $\mathbf{v} = \nabla \times \mathbf{A}$.

The divergence theorem, gives the equivalent integral definition of a _____ field; namely that for any closed surface S, the net total flux through the surface must be zero:

$$\iint_S \mathbf{v} \cdot d\mathbf{s} = 0$$

where $d\mathbf{s}$ is the outward normal to each surface element.

a. Bloch space
b. Trigonometric series
c. Solenoidal
d. Principal part

Chapter 5. Vector Integral Calculus

31. Just as the definite integral of a positive function of one variable represents the area of the region between the graph of the function and the x-axis, the _____ of a positive function of two variables represents the volume of the region between the surface defined by the function (on the three dimensional Cartesian plane where z = f(x,y)) and the plane which contains its domain. (Note that the same volume can be obtained via the triple integral -- the integral of a function in three variables -- of the constant function f(x, y, z) = 1 over the above-mentioned region between the surface and the plane.) If there are more variables, a multiple integral will yield hypervolumes of multi-dimensional functions.
    a. Double integral
    b. Risch algorithm
    c. Constant of integration
    d. Trigonometric substitution

32. _____ can be thought of as energy stored within a physical system. It is called _____ because it has the potential to be converted into other forms of energy, such as kinetic energy, and to do work in the process. The standard (SI) unit of measure for _____ is the joule, the same as for work or energy in general.
    a. Law of Conservation of Energy
    b. BDDC
    c. Potential energy
    d. 15 theorem

33. In physics, _____ is defined as the rate of change of position. it is vector physical quantity; both speed and direction are required to define it. In the SI (metric) system, it is measured in meters per second: (m/s) or ms^{-1}.
    a. Velocity
    b. BIBO stability
    c. 15 theorem
    d. BDDC

34. The _____ of a material is defined as its mass per unit volume. The symbol of _____ is ρ '>rho.)

Mathematically:

$$d = \frac{m}{V}$$

where:

    d is the _____,
    m is the mass,
    V is the volume.

    a. BIBO stability
    b. BDDC
    c. 15 theorem
    d. Density

35. The _____ is an important second-order linear partial differential equation that describes the propagation of a variety of waves, such as sound waves, light waves and water waves. It arises in fields such as acoustics, electromagnetics, and fluid dynamics. Historically, the problem of a vibrating string such as that of a musical instrument was studied by Jean le Rond d'Alembert, Leonhard Euler, Daniel Bernoulli, and Joseph-Louis Lagrange.
    a. Volume
    b. Wave equation
    c. Dirac equation
    d. Lagrangian

36. Typically the pair u and v are taken to be the real and imaginary parts of a complex-valued function f(x + iy) = u(x,y) + iv (x,y.) Suppose that u and v are continuously differentiable on an open subset of C. Then f = u+iv is holomorphic if and only if the partial derivatives of u and v satisfy the _____ and (1b.)

The equations are one way of looking at the condition on a function to be differentiable (holomorphic) in the sense of complex analysis: in other words they encapsulate the notion of function of a complex variable by means of conventional differential calculus.

- a. Cauchy-Riemann equations
- b. Viscosity solution
- c. Solid harmonics
- d. Spherical harmonics

37. In mathematics, specifically in calculus and complex analysis, the _____ of a function f is defined by the formula

$$\frac{f'}{f}$$

where f ' is the derivative of f.

When f is a function f(x) of a real variable x, and takes real, strictly positive values, this is indeed the formula for (log f)', that is, the derivative of the natural logarithm of f, as follows directly from the chain rule.

Many properties of the real logarithm also apply to the _____, even when the function does not take values in the positive reals.

- a. Directional derivative
- b. Logarithmic derivative
- c. Point of inflection
- d. Lin-Tsien equation

38. In mathematics, the _____ is an operator in vector calculus that acts as the inverse to the negative Laplacian, on functions that are smooth and decay rapidly enough at infinity. In its general nature, it is a singular integral operator, defined by convolution with a function having a mathematical singularity at the origin, the Newtonian kernel G which is the fundamental solution of the Laplace equation.

Stating its property in another way, the _____ applied to a function f satisfies Poisson's equation with f as RHS.

- a. Hilbert transform
- b. Kelvin transform
- c. Harmonic function
- d. Newtonian potential

39. In infinitesimal calculus, a _____ is traditionally an infinitesimally small change in a variable. For example, if x is a variable, then a change in the value of x is often denoted Δx (or δx when this change is considered to be small.) The _____ dx represents such a change, but is infinitely small.
- a. Local maximum
- b. The Method of Mechanical Theorems
- c. Dirichlet integral
- d. Differential

40. In the mathematical fields of differential geometry and tensor calculus, differential forms are an approach to multivariable calculus that is independent of coordinates. A _____ of degree k, or (differential) k-form, on a smooth manifold M is a smooth section of the kth exterior power of the cotangent bundle of M. The set of all k-forms on M is a vector space commonly denoted $\Omega^k(M)$.

A differential 0-form is by definition a smooth function on M. A differential 1-form is an object dual to a vector field on M.

    a. Two-form
    c. Hodge dual
    b. Differential form
    d. Soldering

41. In geometry, the _____ (or simply the tangent) to a curve at a given point is the straight line that 'just touches' the curve at that point (in the sense explained more precisely below.) As it passes through the point of tangency, the _____ is 'going in the same direction' as the curve, and in this sense it is the best straight-line approximation to the curve at that point. The same definition applies to space curves and curves in n-dimensional Euclidean space.

    a. Lie derivative
    c. Tangent line
    b. Minimal surface
    d. North pole

Chapter 6. Infinite Series

1. Cantor defined two kinds of _____ numbers, the ordinal numbers and the cardinal numbers. Ordinal numbers may be identified with well-ordered sets, or counting carried on to any stopping point, including points after an _____ number have already been counted. Generalizing finite and the ordinary _____ sequences which are maps from the positive integers leads to mappings from ordinal numbers, and transfinite sequences.
   a. AUSM
   b. ACTRAN
   c. Infinite
   d. ALGOR

2. The terms of the series are often produced according to a certain rule, such as by a formula, by an algorithm, by a sequence of measurements, or even by a random number generator. As there are an infinite number of terms, this notion is often called an _____. Unlike finite summations, series need tools from mathematical analysis to be fully understood and manipulated.
   a. Extreme Value Theorem
   b. Integration by substitution
   c. Infinite series
   d. Extreme value

3. In mathematics, a _____ is an ordered list of objects (or events). Like a set, it contains members (also called elements or terms), and the number of terms (possibly infinite) is called the length of the _____. Unlike a set, order matters, and the exact same elements can appear multiple times at different positions in the _____.
   a. 15 theorem
   b. Y-intercept
   c. Slope
   d. Sequence

4. A _____ of a function of two variables is a curve along which the function has a constant value. In cartography, a _____ (often just called a 'contour') joins points of equal elevation (height) above a given level, such as mean sea level. A contour map is a map illustrated with contour lines, for example a topographic map, which thus shows valleys and hills, and the steepness of slopes.
   a. BIBO stability
   b. BDDC
   c. Contour line
   d. 15 theorem

5. In mathematics, the concept of a '_____' is used to describe the behavior of a function as its argument or input either 'gets close' to some point, or as the argument becomes arbitrarily large; or the behavior of a sequence's elements as their index increases indefinitely. Limits are used in calculus and other branches of mathematical analysis to define derivatives and continuity.

   In formulas, _____ is usually abbreviated as lim

   a. BIBO stability
   b. BDDC
   c. 15 theorem
   d. Limit

6. In mathematics, a _____ is a function for which, intuitively, small changes in the input result in small changes in the output. Otherwise, a function is said to be discontinuous. A _____ with a continuous inverse function is called bicontinuous. An intuitive though imprecise (and inexact) idea of continuity is given by the common statement that a _____ is a function whose graph can be drawn without lifting the chalk from the blackboard.
   a. Hyperbolic angle
   b. Binomial series
   c. Continuous function
   d. Visual Calculus

7. Call S_N the _____ to N of the sequence $\{a_n\}$, or _____ of the series. A series is the sequence of partial sums, $\{S_N\}$.

Chapter 6. Infinite Series

When talking about series, one can refer either to the sequence $\{S_N\}$ of the partial sums, or to the sum of the series,

$$\sum_{n=0}^{\infty} a_n$$

i.e., the limit of the sequence of partial sums - it is clear which one is meant from context.

a. The Method of Mechanical Theorems
b. Maxima
c. Dirichlet integral
d. Partial sum

8. In mathematics, a series (or sometimes also an integral) is said to converge absolutely if the sum (or integral) of the absolute value of the summand or integrand is finite.

More precisely, a real or complex-valued series $\sum_{n=0}^{\infty} a_n$ is said to converge absolutely if $\sum_{n=0}^{\infty} |a_n| < \infty$.

_____ is vitally important to the study of infinite series because on the one hand, it is strong enough that such series retain certain basic properties of finite sums -- the most important ones being rearrangement of the terms and convergence of products of two infinite series -- that are unfortunately not possessed by all convergent series. On the other hand _____ is weak enough to occur very often in practice.

a. Eisenstein series
b. Alternating series test
c. ACTRAN
d. Absolute convergence

9. A _____ of an oscillating system is a pattern of motion in which all parts of the system move sinusoidally with the same frequency. The frequencies of the normal modes of a system are known as its natural frequencies or resonant frequencies. A physical object, such as a building or a bridge or a molecule, has a set of normal modes that depend on its structure and composition.

a. Boundary value problem
b. Phase plane
c. Power series method
d. Normal mode

10. In mathematics, the _____ test for divergence is a simple test for the divergence of an infinite series:

- If $\lim_{n \to \infty} a_n \neq 0$ or if the limit does not exist, then $\sum_{n=1}^{\infty} a_n$ diverges.

Many authors do not name this test or give it a shorter name.

Chapter 6. Infinite Series

Unlike stronger convergence tests, the term test cannot prove by itself that a series converges. In particular, the converse to the test is not true; instead all one can say is:

- If $\lim_{n\to\infty} a_n = 0$, then $\sum_{n=1}^{\infty} a_n$ may or may not converge. In other words, if $\lim_{n\to\infty} a_n = 0$, the test is inconclusive.

The harmonic series is a classic example of a divergent series whose terms limit to zero. The more general class of p-series,

$$\sum_{n=1}^{\infty} \frac{1}{n^p},$$

exemplifies the possible results of the test:

- If $p \le 0$, then the term test identifies the series as divergent.
- If $0 < p \le 1$, then the term test is inconclusive, but the series is divergent by the integral test for convergence.
- If $1 < p$, then the term test is inconclusive, but the series is convergent, again by the integral test for convergence.

The test is typically proved in contrapositive form:

- If $\sum_{n=1}^{\infty} a_n$ converges, then $\lim_{n\to\infty} a_n = 0$.

If s_n are the partial sums of the series, then the assumption that the series converges means that

$$\lim_{n\to\infty} s_n = s$$

for some number s. Then

$$\lim_{n\to\infty} a_n = \lim_{n\to\infty} (s_n - s_{n-1}) = s - s = 0.$$

Chapter 6. Infinite Series

The assumption that the series converges means that it passes Cauchy's convergence test: for every $\varepsilon > 0$ there is a number N such that

$$|a_{n+1} + a_{n+2} + \ldots + a_{n+p}| < \varepsilon$$

holds for all n > N and p ≥ 1. Setting p = 1 recovers the definition of the statement

$$\lim_{n \to \infty} a_n = 0.$$

The simplest version of the term test applies to infinite series of real numbers.

a. Nth term
b. Slope field
c. Leibniz differential
d. Minimum

11. In mathematics, the nth _____ for divergence is a simple test for the divergence of an infinite series:

- If $\lim_{n \to \infty} a_n \neq 0$ or if the limit does not exist, then $\sum_{n=1}^{\infty} a_n$ diverges.

Many authors do not name this test or give it a shorter name.

Unlike stronger convergence tests, the _____ cannot prove by itself that a series converges. In particular, the converse to the test is not true; instead all one can say is:

- If $\lim_{n \to \infty} a_n = 0$, then $\sum_{n=1}^{\infty} a_n$ may or may not converge. In other words, if $\lim_{n \to \infty} a_n = 0$, the test is inconclusive.

The harmonic series is a classic example of a divergent series whose terms limit to zero. The more general class of p-series,

$$\sum_{n=1}^{\infty} \frac{1}{n^p},$$

Chapter 6. Infinite Series

exemplifies the possible results of the test:

- If p ≤ 0, then the _____ identifies the series as divergent.
- If 0 < p ≤ 1, then the _____ is inconclusive, but the series is divergent by the integral test for convergence.
- If 1 < p, then the _____ is inconclusive, but the series is convergent, again by the integral test for convergence.

The test is typically proved in contrapositive form:

- If $\sum_{n=1}^{\infty} a_n$ converges, then $\lim_{n \to \infty} a_n = 0$.

If s_n are the partial sums of the series, then the assumption that the series converges means that

$$\lim_{n \to \infty} s_n = s$$

for some number s. Then

$$\lim_{n \to \infty} a_n = \lim_{n \to \infty} (s_n - s_{n-1}) = s - s = 0.$$

The assumption that the series converges means that it passes Cauchy's convergence test: for every $\varepsilon > 0$ there is a number N such that

$$|a_{n+1} + a_{n+2} + \ldots + a_{n+p}| < \varepsilon$$

holds for all n > N and p ≥ 1. Setting p = 1 recovers the definition of the statement

$$\lim_{n \to \infty} a_n = 0.$$

The simplest version of the _____ applies to infinite series of real numbers.

a. Local minimum
c. Maxima

b. Differential
d. Term test

12. In mathematics, the _____, sometimes called the direct _____ is a criterion for convergence or divergence of a series whose terms are real or complex numbers. The test determines convergence by comparing the terms of the series in question with those of a series whose convergence properties are known.

The _____ states that if the series

$$\sum_{n=1}^{\infty} b_n$$

is an absolutely convergent series and

$$|a_n| \leq |b_n|$$

for sufficiently large n , then the series

$$\sum_{n=1}^{\infty} a_n$$

converges absolutely.

a. Telescoping series
c. Ratio test
b. Conditionally convergent
d. Comparison test

13. In mathematics, a series or integral is said to be _____ if it converges, but it does not converge absolutely. More precisely, a series $\sum_{n=0}^{\infty} a_n$ is said to converge conditionally if $\lim_{m \to \infty} \sum_{n=0}^{m} a_n$ exists and is a finite number (not ∞ or −∞), but $\sum_{n=0}^{\infty} |a_n| = \infty$.

A classical example is given by

$$1 - \frac{1}{2} + \frac{1}{3} - \frac{1}{4} + \frac{1}{5} - \cdots = \sum_{n=1}^{\infty} \frac{(-1)^{n+1}}{n}$$

which converges to ln 2 , but is not absolutely convergent

The simplest examples of _____ series (including the one above) are the alternating series.

a. Ratio test
c. Conditionally convergent
b. Converge absolutely
d. Geometric series

14. Integration is an important concept in mathematics, specifically in the field of calculus and, more broadly, mathematical analysis. Given a function f of a real variable x and an interval [a, b] of the real line, the _____

$$\int_a^b f(x)\,dx,$$

is defined informally to be the net signed area of the region in the xy-plane bounded by the graph of f, the x-axis, and the vertical lines x = a and x = b.

The term '_____' may also refer to the notion of antiderivative, a function F whose derivative is the given function f.

a. Integrand
b. Integral
c. Indefinite integral
d. Integral test for convergence

15. In mathematics, a _____ is a series with a constant ratio between successive terms. For example, the series

$$\frac{1}{2} + \frac{1}{4} + \frac{1}{8} + \frac{1}{16} + \cdots$$

is geometric, because each term is equal to half of the previous term. The sum of this series is 1, as illustrated in the following picture:

_____ are one of the simplest examples of infinite series with finite sums.

a. Converge absolutely
b. Geometric series
c. Sequence transformation
d. Conditionally convergent

16. In acoustics and telecommunication, a _____ of a wave is a component frequency of the signal that is an integer multiple of the fundamental frequency. For example, if the fundamental frequency is f, the harmonics have frequencies f, 2f, 3f, 4f, etc. The harmonics have the property that they are all periodic at the fundamental frequency, therefore the sum of harmonics is also periodic at that frequency.

a. BDDC
b. Harmonic
c. BIBO stability
d. 15 theorem

17. In mathematics, mathematical physics and the theory of stochastic processes, a _____ is a twice continuously differentiable function f : U → R (where U is an open subset of R^n) which satisfies Laplace's equation, i.e.

$$\frac{\partial^2 f}{\partial x_1^2} + \frac{\partial^2 f}{\partial x_2^2} + \cdots + \frac{\partial^2 f}{\partial x_n^2} = 0$$

everywhere on U. This is also often written as

$$\nabla^2 f = 0 \quad \text{or} \quad \Delta f = 0.$$

Chapter 6. Infinite Series

There also exists a seemingly weaker definition that is equivalent. Indeed a function is harmonic if and only if it is weakly harmonic.

Harmonic functions can be defined on an arbitrary Riemannian manifold, using the Laplace-de Rham operator Δ.

a. Pluriharmonic function
b. Maximum principle
c. Kelvin transform
d. Harmonic function

18. A _____ is an expression which compares quantities relative to each other. The most common examples involve two quantities, but in theory any number of quantities can be compared. In mathematical terms, they are represented by separating each quantity with a colon, for example the _____ 2:3, which is read as the _____ 'two to three'.

a. 15 theorem
b. Sequence
c. Y-intercept
d. Ratio

19. In mathematics, the _____ is a test (or 'criterion') for the convergence of a series

$$\sum_{n=0}^{\infty} a_n$$

whose terms are real or complex numbers. The test was first published by Jean le Rond d'Alembert and is sometimes known as d'Alembert's _____. The test makes use of the number

()

in the cases where this limit exists.

a. Converge absolutely
b. Telescoping series
c. Geometric series
d. Ratio test

20. In mathematics, an _____ is an infinite series of the form

$$\sum_{n=0}^{\infty} (-1)^n a_n,$$

with $a_n \geq 0$ (or $a_n \leq 0$) for all n. A finite sum of this kind is an alternating sum. An _____ converges if the terms a_n converge to 0 monotonically.

a. Extreme value
b. Infinite series
c. Uniform convergence
d. Alternating series

21. The _____ is a method used to prove that infinite series of terms converge. It was discovered by Gottfried Leibniz and is sometimes known as Leibniz's test or the Leibniz criterion.

A series of the form

$$\sum_{n=1}^{\infty}(-1)^n a_n$$

where all the a_n are positive or 0, is called an alternating series.

a. Alternating series test
b. Absolute convergence
c. ACTRAN
d. Eisenstein series

22. In mathematics, the _____ is a criterion for the convergence (a convergence test) of an infinite series

$$\sum_{n=1}^{\infty} a_n.$$

It is particularly useful in connection with power series.

The _____ was developed first by Cauchy and so is sometimes known as the Cauchy _____ or Cauchy's radical test.
The _____ uses the number

$$C = \limsup_{n \to \infty} \sqrt[n]{|a_n|},$$

where 'lim sup' denotes the limit superior, possibly ∞.

a. Root test
b. Racetrack principle
c. Mean Value Theorem
d. Related rates

23. A _____ is a set of standard clothing worn by members of an organization while participating in that organization's activity. Modern uniforms are worn by armed forces and paramilitary organisations such as police, emergency services, security guards, in some workplaces and schools and by inmates in prisons. In some countries, some other officials also wear uniforms in their duties; such is the case of the Commissioned Corps of the United States Public Health Service or the French prefects.

a. AUSM
b. ACTRAN
c. Uniform
d. ALGOR

24. In mathematics, a function f is uniformly continuous if, roughly speaking, it is possible to guarantee that $f(x)$ and $f(y)$ be as close to each other as we please by requiring only that x and y are sufficiently close to each other; unlike ordinary continuity, the maximum distance between $f(x)$ and $f(y)$ cannot depend on x and y themselves. For instance, any isometry (distance-preserving map) between metric spaces is uniformly continuous.

_____, unlike continuity, is meaningless in an arbitrary topological space, since it relies on the ability to compare the sizes of neighbourhoods of distinct points of a space.

   a. ACTRAN   b. ALGOR
   c. Uniform continuity   d. AUSM

25. In mathematics, given a subset S of a partially ordered set T, the _____ (sup) of S, if it exists, is the least element of T that is greater than or equal to each element of S. Consequently, the _____ is also referred to as the least upper bound, lub or LUB. If the _____ exists, it may or may not belong to S.
   a. BDDC   b. BIBO stability
   c. 15 theorem   d. Supremum

26. In mathematics, especially in order theory, an _____ of a subset S of some partially ordered set (P, >≤) is an element of P which is greater than or equal to every element of S. The term lower bound is defined dually as an element of P which is lesser than or equal to every element of S. A set with an _____ is said to be bounded from above by that bound, a set with a lower bound is said to be bounded from below by that bound.

A subset S of a partially ordered set P may fail to have any bounds or may have many different upper and lower bounds. By transitivity, any element greater than or equal to an _____ of S is again an _____ of S, and any element lesser than or equal to any lower bound of S is again a lower bound of S. This leads to the consideration of least upper bounds: (or suprema) and greatest lower bounds (or infima.)

   a. Upper bound   b. ALGOR
   c. ACTRAN   d. AUSM

27. In mathematics, the _____ is an analogue of the comparison test for infinite series, and applies to a series whose terms are themselves functions with real or complex values.

Suppose $\{f_n\}$ is a sequence of real- or complex-valued functions defined on a set A, and that there exist positive constants M_n such that

for all n>≥1 and all x in A. Suppose further that the series

converges.

   a. 15 theorem   b. BDDC
   c. BIBO stability   d. Weierstrass M-test

Chapter 6. Infinite Series

28. In calculus, a branch of mathematics, the _____ is a measurement of how a function changes when its input changes. Loosely speaking, a _____ can be thought of as how much a quantity is changing at some given point. For example, the _____ of the position (or distance) of a vehicle with respect to time is the instantaneous velocity (respectively, instantaneous speed) at which the vehicle is traveling.

The process of finding a _____ is called differentiation. The fundamental theorem of calculus states that differentiation is the reverse process to integration.

    a. Bounded function
    b. Stationary phase approximation
    c. Semi-differentiability
    d. Derivative

29. In mathematics, the _____ of a power series is a non-negative quantity, either a real number or ∞, that represents a domain (within the radius) in which the series will converge. Within the _____, a power series converges absolutely and uniformly on compacta as well. If the series converges, it is the Taylor series of the analytic function to which it converges inside its _____.

    a. Holomorphically separable
    b. Radius of convergence
    c. Branch point
    d. Blaschke product

30. In elementary algebra, a _____ is a polynomial with two terms--the sum of two monomials--often bound by parenthesis or brackets when operated upon. It is the simplest kind of polynomial other than monomials.

- The _____ $a^2 - b^2$ can be factored as the product of two other binomials:

    $a^2 - b^2 = (a + b)(a - b.)$

    This is a special case of the more general formula:

    $$a^{n+1} - b^{n+1} = (a - b) \sum_{k=0}^{n} a^k b^{n-k}.$$

- The product of a pair of linear binomials $(ax + b)$ and $(cx + d)$ is:

    $(ax + b)(cx + d) = acx^2 + axd + bcx + bd.$

- A _____ raised to the nth power, represented as

    $(a + b)^n$

    can be expanded by means of the _____ theorem or, equivalently, using Pascal's triangle. Taking a simple example, the perfect square _____ $(p + q)^2$ can be found by squaring the first digit, adding twice the product of the first and second digit and finally adding the square of the second digit, to give $p^2 + 2pq + q^2$.

    a. Completing the square
    b. Partial fractions
    c. Multinomial theorem
    d. Binomial

31. In mathematics, the _____ $\binom{n}{k}$ is the coefficient of the x^k term in the polynomial expansion of the binomial power $(1 + x)^n$.

Chapter 6. Infinite Series

In combinatorics, $\binom{n}{k}$ is interpreted as the number of k-element subsets (the k-combinations) of an n-element set, that is the number of ways that k things can be 'chosen' from a set of n things. Hence, $\binom{n}{k}$ is often read as 'n choose k' and is called the choose function of n and k.

    a. 15 theorem   b. Binomial coefficient
    c. Factorial   d. BDDC

32. In mathematics, a _____ is a constant multiplicative factor of a certain object. For example, in the expression $9x^2$, the _____ of x^2 is 9.

The object can be such things as a variable, a vector, a function, etc.

    a. Degree of the polynomial   b. Resultant
    c. Binomial type   d. Coefficient

33. In mathematics, the _____ is a representation of a function as an infinite sum of terms calculated from the values of its derivatives at a single point. It may be regarded as the limit of the Taylor polynomials. If the series is centered at zero, the series is also called a Maclaurin series.
    a. BDDC   b. Taylor series
    c. BIBO stability   d. 15 theorem

34. In mathematics, an _____ is a function that is locally given by a convergent power series. Analytic functions can be thought of as a bridge between polynomials and general functions. There exist both real analytic functions and complex analytic functions, categories that are similar in some ways, but different in others.
    a. Upper half-plane   b. Imaginary number
    c. Euler's formula   d. Analytic function

35. The _____ is a function in mathematics. The application of this function to a value x is written as exp(x). Equivalently, this can be written in the form e^x, where e is a mathematical constant, the base of the natural logarithm, which equals approximately 2.718281828, and is also known as Euler's number.
    a. ACTRAN   b. Exponential function
    c. Integral part   d. Area hyperbolic functions

36. In mathematics, the _____ of a function y = f(x) is a function that, in some fashion, 'undoes' the effect of f The _____ of f is denoted f^{-1}. The statements y=f(x) and $x=f^{-1}(y)$ are equivalent.
    a. ALGOR   b. ACTRAN
    c. AUSM   d. Inverse

37. In mathematics, if f is a function from A to B then an _____ for f is a function in the opposite direction, from B to A, with the property that a round trip (a composition) from A to B to A (or from B to A to B) returns each element of the initial set to itself. Thus, if an input x into the function f produces an output y, then inputting y into the _____ f^{-1} (read f inverse, not to be confused with exponentiation) produces the output x. Not every function has an inverse; those that do are called invertible.

Chapter 6. Infinite Series

a. Augustin Louis Cauchy
c. Inverse function
b. Augustin-Jean Fresnel
d. Aristotle

38. In mathematics, the _____ (or modulus) of a real number is its numerical value without regard to its sign. So, for example, 3 is the _____ of both 3 and −3.

The _____ of a number a is denoted by $|a|$.

a. ACTRAN
c. Absolute value
b. Area hyperbolic functions
d. Exponential function

39. In mathematics, the complex numbers are an extension of the real numbers obtained by adjoining an imaginary unit, denoted i.

Every _____ can be written in the form a + bi, where a and b are real numbers called the real part and the imaginary part of the _____, respectively.

Complex numbers are a field, and thus have addition, subtraction, multiplication, and division operations. These operations extend the corresponding operations on real numbers, although with a number of additional elegant and useful properties, e.g., negative real numbers can be obtained by squaring complex (imaginary) numbers.

a. Real part
c. Conjugated line
b. Complex number
d. Filled Julia set

40. In probability theory and statistics, the _____ (or expectation value or mean and for continuous random variables with a density function it is the probability density -weighted integral of the possible values.

The term '_____' can be misleading.

a. ACTRAN
c. AUSM
b. ALGOR
d. Expected value

41. In mathematics, _____ and minima, known collectively as extrema, are the largest value (maximum) or smallest value (minimum), that a function takes in a point either within a given neighbourhood (local extremum) or on the function domain in its entirety (global extremum.)

Throughout, a point refers to an input (x), while a value refers to an output (y): one distinguishing between the maximum value and the point (or points) at which it occurs.

A real-valued function f defined on the real line is said to have a local maximum point at the point x^*, if there exists some $\varepsilon > 0$, such that $f(x^*) \geq f(x)$ when $|x - x^*| < \varepsilon$.

a. Related rates
c. Racetrack principle
b. Leibniz formula
d. Maxima

Chapter 6. Infinite Series

42. In geometry, for a finite planar surface of scalar area S, the vector area

S

is defined as a vector whose magnitude is S and whose direction is perpendicular to the plane, as determined by the right hand rule on the rim (moving one's right hand counterclockwise around the rim, when the palm of the hand is 'touching' the surface, and the straight thumb indicate the direction.)

$$\mathbf{S} = \hat{\mathbf{n}} S$$

This can only be defined for flat surfaces, or for regions of curved surfaces which are sufficiently small that they can be considered flat.

The concept of an _____ simplifies the equation for determining the flux through the surface.

    a. ALGOR   b. Area vector
    c. Orthogonal trajectories   d. ACTRAN

43. In elementary mathematics, physics, and engineering, a _____ is a geometric object that has both a magnitude (or length), direction and sense, (i.e., orientation along the given direction.) A _____ is frequently represented by a line segment with a definite direction, or graphically as an arrow, connecting an initial point A with a terminal point B, and denoted by

The magnitude of the _____ is the length of the segment and the direction characterizes the displacement of B relative to A: how much one should move the point A to 'carry' it to the point B.

Many algebraic operations on real numbers have close analogues for vectors.

    a. Vector   b. Linear partial differential operator
    c. BDDC   d. 15 theorem

44. In calculus, an _____ is the limit of a definite integral as an endpoint of the interval of integration approaches either a specified real number or ∞ or −∞ or, in some cases, as both endpoints approach limits.

Specifically, an _____ is a limit of the form

$$\lim_{b \to \infty} \int_a^b f(x)\, dx, \qquad \lim_{a \to -\infty} \int_a^b f(x)\, dx,$$

or of the form

$$\lim_{c \to b^-} \int_a^c f(x)\, dx, \quad \lim_{c \to a^+} \int_c^b f(x)\, dx,$$

in which one takes a limit in one or the other (or sometimes both) endpoints. Improper integrals may also occur at an interior point of the domain of integration, or at multiple such points.

a. ACTRAN
b. ALGOR
c. AUSM
d. Improper integral

45. In mathematics, the _____ of a non-negative integer n, denoted by n!, is the product of all positive integers less than or equal to n. For example,

$$5! = 1 \times 2 \times 3 \times 4 \times 5 = 120$$

and

$$6! = 1 \times 2 \times 3 \times 4 \times 5 \times 6 = 720.$$

The notation n! was introduced by Christian Kramp in 1808.

The _____ function is formally defined by

$$n! = \prod_{k=1}^{n} k \qquad \forall n \in \mathbb{N}$$

or recursively defined by

$$n! = \begin{cases} n \leq 1 & 1 \\ n > 1 & n(n-1)! \end{cases} \qquad \forall n \in \mathbb{N}.$$

Both of the above definitions incorporate the instance

$$0! = 1$$

as an instance of the fact that the product of no numbers at all is 1.

a. Constraint counting
c. 15 theorem
b. BDDC
d. Factorial

46. In mathematics, the _____ is an extension of the factorial function to real and complex numbers. For a complex number z with positive real part the _____ is defined by

$$\Gamma(z) = \int_0^\infty t^{z-1} e^{-t}\, dt\, .$$

This definition can be extended to the rest of the complex plane, excepting the non-positive integers.

If n is a positive integer, then

Γ(n) = (n − 1)!,

showing the connection to the factorial function.

a. Digamma function
c. Pochhammer k-symbol
b. Multivariate gamma function
d. Gamma function

47. In mathematics, the _____, also called the Euler integral of the first kind, is a special function defined by

$$B(x, y) = \int_0^1 t^{x-1}(1-t)^{y-1}\, dt$$

for $\mathrm{Re}(x), \mathrm{Re}(y) > 0.$

The _____ was studied by Euler and Legendre and was given its name by Jacques Binet.

The _____ is symmetric, meaning that

$$B(x, y) = B(y, x).$$

It has many other forms, including:

$$B(x,y) = \frac{\Gamma(x)\Gamma(y)}{\Gamma(x+y)}$$

$$B(x,y) = 2\int_0^{\pi/2} (\sin\theta)^{2x-1}(\cos\theta)^{2y-1}\,d\theta, \qquad \text{Re}(x) > 0,\ \text{Re}(y) > 0$$

$$B(x,y) = \int_0^\infty \frac{t^{x-1}}{(1+t)^{x+y}}\,dt, \qquad \text{Re}(x) > 0,\ \text{Re}(y) > 0$$

$$B(x,y) = \sum_{n=0}^\infty \frac{\binom{n-y}{n}}{x+n},$$

$$B(x,y) = \prod_{n=0}^\infty \left(1 + \frac{xy}{n(x+y+n)}\right)^{-1},$$

$$B(x,y)\cdot B(x+y, 1-y) = \frac{\pi}{x\sin(\pi y)},$$

where Γ is the gamma function. The second identity shows in particular $\Gamma(1/2) = \sqrt{\pi}$.

a. Pochhammer symbol
b. Multivariate gamma function
c. Pochhammer k-symbol
d. Beta function

48. _____ _____ is a type of motion in which the velocity of an object changes equal amounts in equal time periods. An example of an object having _____ would be a ball rolling down a ramp. The object picks up velocity as it goes down the ramp with equal changes in time.

a. Uniform Acceleration
b. AUSM
c. ACTRAN
d. ALGOR

Chapter 7. Fourier Series and Orthogonal Functions

1. In mathematics, a _____ is a function that repeats its values in regular intervals or periods. The most important examples are the trigonometric functions, which repeat over intervals of length 2π. Periodic functions are used throughout science to describe oscillations, waves, and other phenomena that exhibit periodicity.
   a. Partial sum
   b. Limits of integration
   c. Term test
   d. Periodic function

2. Trigonometry is a branch of mathematics that deals with triangles, particularly those plane triangles in which one angle has 90 degrees (right triangles.) Trigonometry deals with relationships between the sides and the angles of triangles and with the _____ functions, which describe those relationships.

   Trigonometry has applications in both pure mathematics and in applied mathematics, where it is essential in many branches of science and technology.

   a. Trigonometric
   b. Sine
   c. Trigonometric integrals
   d. Trigonometric functions

3. The _____ of an angle is the ratio of the length of the adjacent side to the length of the hypotenuse. In our case

$$\cos A = \frac{\text{adjacent}}{\text{hypotenuse}} = \frac{b}{h}.$$

   The tangent of an angle is the ratio of the length of the opposite side to the length of the adjacent side. In our case

$$\tan A = \frac{\text{opposite}}{\text{adjacent}} = \frac{a}{b}.$$

   The remaining three functions are best defined using the above three functions.

   a. Trigonometric
   b. Trigonometric functions
   c. Sine integral
   d. Cosine

4. In acoustics and telecommunication, a _____ of a wave is a component frequency of the signal that is an integer multiple of the fundamental frequency. For example, if the fundamental frequency is f, the harmonics have frequencies f, 2f, 3f, 4f, etc. The harmonics have the property that they are all periodic at the fundamental frequency, therefore the sum of harmonics is also periodic at that frequency.
   a. Harmonic
   b. BIBO stability
   c. 15 theorem
   d. BDDC

5. In mathematics, mathematical physics and the theory of stochastic processes, a _____ is a twice continuously differentiable function f : U → R (where U is an open subset of R^n) which satisfies Laplace's equation, i.e.

$$\frac{\partial^2 f}{\partial x_1^2} + \frac{\partial^2 f}{\partial x_2^2} + \cdots + \frac{\partial^2 f}{\partial x_n^2} = 0$$

everywhere on U. This is also often written as

$$\nabla^2 f = 0 \quad \text{or} \quad \Delta f = 0.$$

There also exists a seemingly weaker definition that is equivalent. Indeed a function is harmonic if and only if it is weakly harmonic.

Harmonic functions can be defined on an arbitrary Riemannian manifold, using the Laplace-de Rham operator Δ.

a. Pluriharmonic function
b. Maximum principle
c. Kelvin transform
d. Harmonic function

6. In mathematics, the hyperbolic functions are analogs of the ordinary trigonometric functions. The basic hyperbolic functions are the hyperbolic sine 'sinh', and the _____ 'cosh', from which are derived the hyperbolic tangent 'tanh', etc., in analogy to the derived trigonometric functions. The inverse hyperbolic functions are the area hyperbolic sine 'arsinh' (also called 'asinh', or sometimes by the misnomer of 'arcsinh') and so on.

a. Square root function
b. Step function
c. Hyperbolic tangent
d. Hyperbolic cosine

7. A curve γ is said to be closed or a loop if $I = [a, b]$ and if $\gamma(a) = \gamma(b)$. A _____ is thus a continuous mapping of the circle S¹; a simple _____ is also called a Jordan curve or a Jordan arc. The Jordan curve theorem states that such curves divide the plane into an 'interior' and an 'exterior'.

a. Kappa curve
b. Curve
c. Bullet-nose curve
d. Closed curve

8. In mathematics, a (topological) _____ is defined as follows: let I be an interval of real numbers (i.e. a non-empty connected subset of $\mathbb{R}$); then a _____ γ is a continuous mapping $\gamma : I \to X$, where X is a topological space. The _____ γ is said to be simple if it is injective, i.e. if for all x, y in I, we have $\gamma(x) = \gamma(y) \implies x = y$. If I is a closed bounded interval $[a, b]$, we also allow the possibility $\gamma(a) = \gamma(b)$ (this convention makes it possible to talk about closed simple _____.)

a. Tractrix
b. Closed curve
c. Prolate cycloid
d. Curve

9. A _____ is a type of manifold that is locally similar enough to Euclidean space to allow one to do calculus Any manifold can be described by a collection of charts, also known as an atlas.

a. Tangent line
b. Sphere
c. Minimal surface
d. Differentiable manifold

10. In mathematics and statistics, the _____ of a list of numbers is the sum of all of the list divided by the number of items in the list. If the list is a statistical population, then the mean of that population is called a population mean. If the list is a statistical sample, we call the resulting statistic a sample mean.

a. ALGOR
b. AUSM
c. Arithmetic mean
d. ACTRAN

11. In probability theory and statistics, the _____ (or expectation value or mean and for continuous random variables with a density function it is the probability density -weighted integral of the possible values.

The term '_____' can be misleading.

a. Expected value
b. ACTRAN
c. AUSM
d. ALGOR

12. The method of _____ or ordinary _____ is used to solve overdetermined systems. _____ is often applied in statistical contexts, particularly regression analysis.

_____ can be interpreted as a method of fitting data. The best fit in the _____ sense is that instance of the model for which the sum of squared residuals has its least value, a residual being the difference between an observed value and the value given by the model.

a. 15 theorem
b. BIBO stability
c. BDDC
d. Least squares

13. _____ is the magnitude of change in the oscillating variable, with each oscillation, within an oscillating system. For instance, sound waves are oscillations in atmospheric pressure and their amplitudes are proportional to the change in pressure during one oscillation. If the variable undergoes regular oscillations, and a graph of the system is drawn with the oscillating variable as the vertical axis and time as the horizontal axis, the _____ is visually represented by the vertical distance between the extrema of the curve.

a. AUSM
b. ALGOR
c. ACTRAN
d. Amplitude

14. In infinitesimal calculus, a _____ is traditionally an infinitesimally small change in a variable. For example, if x is a variable, then a change in the value of x is often denoted Δx (or δx when this change is considered to be small.) The _____ dx represents such a change, but is infinitely small.

a. Dirichlet integral
b. The Method of Mechanical Theorems
c. Local maximum
d. Differential

15. A _____ is a mathematical equation for an unknown function of one or several variables that relates the values of the function itself and of its derivatives of various orders. they play a prominent role in engineering, physics, economics and other disciplines.

A simplified real world example of a _____ is modeling the acceleration of a ball falling through the air (considering only gravity and air resistance.)

a. Caloric polynomial
b. Phase line
c. Differential equation
d. Structural stability

Chapter 7. Fourier Series and Orthogonal Functions

16. In mathematics, even functions and odd functions are functions which satisfy particular symmetry relations, with respect to taking additive inverses. They are important in many areas of mathematical analysis, especially the theory of power series and Fourier series. They are named for the parity of the powers of the power functions which satisfy each condition: the function f(x) = x^n is an _____ if n is an even integer, and it is an odd function if n is an odd integer.
   a. Operational calculus
   b. Infinite series
   c. Even function
   d. Integral of secant cubed

17. In mathematics, even functions and odd functions are functions which satisfy particular symmetry relations, with respect to taking additive inverses. They are important in many areas of mathematical analysis, especially the theory of power series and Fourier series. They are named for the parity of the powers of the power functions which satisfy each condition: the function f(x) = x^n is an even function if n is an even integer, and it is an _____ if n is an odd integer.
   a. Integration by substitution
   b. Even function
   c. Integral of secant cubed
   d. Odd function

18. The _____ of an angle is the ratio of the length of the opposite side to the length of the hypotenuse. In our case

$$\sin A = \frac{\text{opposite}}{\text{hypotenuse}} = \frac{a}{h}.$$

Note that this ratio does not depend on size of the particular right triangle chosen, as long as it contains the angle A, since all such triangles are similar.

The cosine of an angle is the ratio of the length of the adjacent side to the length of the hypotenuse.

   a. Trigonometric
   b. Sine integral
   c. Trigonometric functions
   d. Sine

19. _____ is any physical or virtual entity that is owned by an individual or jointly by a group of individuals. An owner of _____ has the right to consume, sell, rent, mortgage, transfer and exchange his or her _____. Important widely-recognized types of _____ include real _____, personal _____ (other physical possessions), and intellectual _____ (rights over artistic creations, inventions, etc.), although the latter is not always as widely recognized or enforced.
   a. 15 theorem
   b. BDDC
   c. BIBO stability
   d. Property

20. A _____ is a set of standard clothing worn by members of an organization while participating in that organization's activity. Modern uniforms are worn by armed forces and paramilitary organisations such as police, emergency services, security guards, in some workplaces and schools and by inmates in prisons. In some countries, some other officials also wear uniforms in their duties; such is the case of the Commissioned Corps of the United States Public Health Service or the French prefects.
   a. Uniform
   b. AUSM
   c. ACTRAN
   d. ALGOR

Chapter 7. Fourier Series and Orthogonal Functions

21. In mathematics, a function f is uniformly continuous if, roughly speaking, it is possible to guarantee that $f(x)$ and $f(y)$ be as close to each other as we please by requiring only that x and y are sufficiently close to each other; unlike ordinary continuity, the maximum distance between $f(x)$ and $f(y)$ cannot depend on x and y themselves. For instance, any isometry (distance-preserving map) between metric spaces is uniformly continuous.

_____, unlike continuity, is meaningless in an arbitrary topological space, since it relies on the ability to compare the sizes of neighbourhoods of distinct points of a space.

a. ALGOR
b. Uniform continuity
c. AUSM
d. ACTRAN

22. In mathematics, two vectors are _____ if they are perpendicular, i.e., they form a right angle. For example, a subway and the street above, although they do not physically intersect, are _____ if they cross at a right angle.

a. Orthogonal
b. ACTRAN
c. AUSM
d. ALGOR

23. In mathematics and its applications, a _____ system is a system for assigning an n-tuple of numbers or scalars to each point in an n-dimensional space. This concept is part of the theory of manifolds. 'Scalars' in many cases means real numbers, but, depending on context, can mean complex numbers or elements of some other commutative ring.

a. Spherical coordinate system
b. 15 theorem
c. Cylindrical coordinate system
d. Coordinate

24. In mathematics, an _____ space is a vector space with the additional structure of _____. This additional structure associates each pair of vectors in the space with a scalar quantity known as the _____ of the vectors. Inner products allow the rigorous introduction of intuitive geometrical notions such as the length of a vector or the angle between two vectors.

a. ALGOR
b. ACTRAN
c. Inner product
d. AUSM

25. In mathematics, an _____ space is a topological space whose dimension is n (where n is a fixed natural number.) The archetypical example is _____ Euclidean space, which describes Euclidean geometry in n dimensions.

Many familiar geometric objects can be generalized to any number of dimensions.

a. 15 theorem
b. N-dimensional
c. BIBO stability
d. BDDC

26. In computer science and information science, _____ could also be a method or an algorithm. Again, an example will illustrate: There are systems of counting, as with Roman numerals, and various systems for filing papers, or catalogues, and various library systems, of which the Dewey Decimal _____ is an example. This still fits with the definition of components which are connected together (in this case in order to facilitate the flow of information.)

a. BDDC
b. 15 theorem
c. BIBO stability
d. System

Chapter 7. Fourier Series and Orthogonal Functions

27. In elementary mathematics, physics, and engineering, a _____ is a geometric object that has both a magnitude (or length), direction and sense, (i.e., orientation along the given direction.) A _____ is frequently represented by a line segment with a definite direction, or graphically as an arrow, connecting an initial point A with a terminal point B, and denoted by

>

The magnitude of the _____ is the length of the segment and the direction characterizes the displacement of B relative to A: how much one should move the point A to 'carry' it to the point B.

Many algebraic operations on real numbers have close analogues for vectors.

a. BDDC
b. Linear partial differential operator
c. 15 theorem
d. Vector

28. For some curves there is a smallest number L that is an upper bound on the length of any polygonal approximation. If such a number exists, then the curve is said to be rectifiable and the curve is defined to have _____ L.

Let C be a curve in Euclidean (or, generally, a metric) space $X = R^n$, so C is the image of a continuous function f : [a, b] → X of the interval [a, b] into X.

a. Integration by parametric derivatives
b. Order of integration
c. Arc length
d. Integrand

29. _____ is the long dimension of any object. The _____ of a thing is the distance between its ends, its linear extent as measured from end to end. This may be distinguished from height, which is vertical extent, and width or breadth, which are the distance from side to side, measuring across the object at right angles to the _____.

a. BDDC
b. BIBO stability
c. 15 theorem
d. Length

30. In mathematics, a _____ in a normed vector space is a vector (often a spatial vector) whose length is 1 (the unit length.) A _____ is often denoted by a lowercase letter with a superscribed caret or e;hate;, like this: $\hat{\imath}$.

In Euclidean space, the dot product of two unit vectors is simply the cosine of the angle between them.

a. Unit vector
b. ALGOR
c. Overdetermined
d. ACTRAN

31. A _____ of a function of two variables is a curve along which the function has a constant value. In cartography, a _____ (often just called a 'contour') joins points of equal elevation (height) above a given level, such as mean sea level. A contour map is a map illustrated with contour lines, for example a topographic map, which thus shows valleys and hills, and the steepness of slopes.

a. 15 theorem
b. BIBO stability
c. BDDC
d. Contour line

32. In calculus, a branch of mathematics, the _____ is a measurement of how a function changes when its input changes. Loosely speaking, a _____ can be thought of as how much a quantity is changing at some given point. For example, the _____ of the position (or distance) of a vehicle with respect to time is the instantaneous velocity (respectively, instantaneous speed) at which the vehicle is traveling.

The process of finding a _____ is called differentiation. The fundamental theorem of calculus states that differentiation is the reverse process to integration.

    a. Semi-differentiability
    b. Bounded function
    c. Stationary phase approximation
    d. Derivative

33. Integration is an important concept in mathematics, specifically in the field of calculus and, more broadly, mathematical analysis. Given a function f of a real variable x and an interval [a, b] of the real line, the _____

$$\int_a^b f(x)\,dx,$$

is defined informally to be the net signed area of the region in the xy-plane bounded by the graph of f, the x-axis, and the vertical lines x = a and x = b.

The term '_____' may also refer to the notion of antiderivative, a function F whose derivative is the given function f.

    a. Indefinite integral
    b. Integral test for convergence
    c. Integrand
    d. Integral

34. A _____ is a mathematical device used when performing a sum, integral, or average in order to give some elements more 'weight' or influence on the result than other elements in the same set. They occur frequently in statistics and analysis, and are closely related to the concept of a measure. They can be constructed in both discrete and continuous settings.

    a. 15 theorem
    b. Weight function
    c. BDDC
    d. BIBO stability

35. In geometry, for a finite planar surface of scalar area S, the vector area

$$\mathbf{S}$$

is defined as a vector whose magnitude is S and whose direction is perpendicular to the plane, as determined by the right hand rule on the rim (moving one's right hand counterclockwise around the rim, when the palm of the hand is 'touching' the surface, and the straight thumb indicate the direction.)

$$\mathbf{S} = \hat{\mathbf{n}} S$$

This can only be defined for flat surfaces, or for regions of curved surfaces which are sufficiently small that they can be considered flat.

Chapter 7. Fourier Series and Orthogonal Functions

The concept of an _____ simplifies the equation for determining the flux through the surface.

a. Orthogonal trajectories
c. ACTRAN
b. ALGOR
d. Area vector

36. In mathematics, a _____ decomposes a periodic function into a sum of simple oscillating functions, namely sines and cosines (or complex exponentials.) The study of _____ is a branch of Fourier analysis. _____ were introduced by Joseph Fourier (1768-1830) for the purpose of solving the heat equation in a metal plate.

a. BIBO stability
c. BDDC
b. 15 theorem
d. Fourier series

37. The _____ of a material is defined as its mass per unit volume. The symbol of _____ is ρ '>rho.)

Mathematically:

$$d = \frac{m}{V}$$

where:

d is the _____,
m is the mass,
V is the volume.

a. Density
c. 15 theorem
b. BDDC
d. BIBO stability

38. The _____ is an important partial differential equation which describes the distribution of heat (or variation in temperature) in a given region over time. For a function u(x,y,z,t) of three spatial variables (x,y,z) and the time variable t, the _____ is

$$\frac{\partial u}{\partial t} - k \left(\frac{\partial^2 u}{\partial x^2} + \frac{\partial^2 u}{\partial y^2} + \frac{\partial^2 u}{\partial z^2} \right) = 0$$

or equivalently

$$\frac{\partial u}{\partial t} = k \nabla^2 u$$

where k is a constant.

The _____ is of fundamental importance in diverse scientific fields.

a. Heat equation
b. 15 theorem
c. BIBO stability
d. BDDC

Chapter 8. Functions of a Complex Variable

1. In mathematics, the complex numbers are an extension of the real numbers obtained by adjoining an imaginary unit, denoted i.

    Every _____ can be written in the form a + bi, where a and b are real numbers called the real part and the imaginary part of the _____, respectively.

    Complex numbers are a field, and thus have addition, subtraction, multiplication, and division operations. These operations extend the corresponding operations on real numbers, although with a number of additional elegant and useful properties, e.g., negative real numbers can be obtained by squaring complex (imaginary) numbers.

    a. Real part
    b. Filled Julia set
    c. Conjugated line
    d. Complex number

2. In mathematics, the _____ of a complex number z, is the first element of the ordered pair of real numbers representing z, i.e. if z = (x,y), or equivalently, z = x + iy, then the _____ of z is x. It is denoted by Re{z} or $\mathfrak{R}\{z\}$, where $\mathfrak{R}$ is a capital R in the Fraktur typeface. The complex function which maps z to the _____ of z is not holomorphic.

    a. Conjugated line
    b. Filled Julia set
    c. Complex number
    d. Real part

3. In computer science and information science, _____ could also be a method or an algorithm. Again, an example will illustrate: There are systems of counting, as with Roman numerals, and various systems for filing papers, or catalogues, and various library systems, of which the Dewey Decimal _____ is an example. This still fits with the definition of components which are connected together (in this case in order to facilitate the flow of information.)

    a. BIBO stability
    b. BDDC
    c. 15 theorem
    d. System

4. In mathematics, the _____ (or modulus) of a real number is its numerical value without regard to its sign. So, for example, 3 is the _____ of both 3 and −3.

    The _____ of a number a is denoted by $|a|$.

    a. Area hyperbolic functions
    b. Absolute value
    c. ACTRAN
    d. Exponential function

5. In mathematics, the _____ of a complex number is given by changing the sign of the imaginary part. Thus, the conjugate of the complex number

$$z = a + ib$$

(where a and b are real numbers) is

$$\overline{z} = a - ib.$$

The _____ is also very commonly denoted by z * . Here $\bar{z}$ is chosen to avoid confusion with the notation for the conjugate transpose of a matrix (which can be thought of as a generalization of complex conjugation.)

a. Filled Julia set
b. Conjugated line
c. Complex conjugate
d. Complex number

6. The _____ is a function in mathematics. The application of this function to a value x is written as exp(x). Equivalently, this can be written in the form e^x, where e is a mathematical constant, the base of the natural logarithm, which equals approximately 2.718281828, and is also known as Euler's number.

a. Exponential function
b. Integral part
c. ACTRAN
d. Area hyperbolic functions

7. Trigonometry is a branch of mathematics that deals with triangles, particularly those plane triangles in which one angle has 90 degrees (right triangles.) Trigonometry deals with relationships between the sides and the angles of triangles and with the _____ functions, which describe those relationships.

Trigonometry has applications in both pure mathematics and in applied mathematics, where it is essential in many branches of science and technology.

a. Trigonometric
b. Sine
c. Trigonometric integrals
d. Trigonometric functions

8. In mathematics, an _____ is a function that is locally given by a convergent power series. Analytic functions can be thought of as a bridge between polynomials and general functions. There exist both real analytic functions and complex analytic functions, categories that are similar in some ways, but different in others.

a. Euler's formula
b. Imaginary number
c. Analytic function
d. Upper half-plane

9. In mathematics, a _____ is a function for which, intuitively, small changes in the input result in small changes in the output. Otherwise, a function is said to be discontinuous. A _____ with a continuous inverse function is called bicontinuous. An intuitive though imprecise (and inexact) idea of continuity is given by the common statement that a _____ is a function whose graph can be drawn without lifting the chalk from the blackboard.

a. Continuous function
b. Hyperbolic angle
c. Visual Calculus
d. Binomial series

10. In elementary mathematics, physics, and engineering, a _____ is a geometric object that has both a magnitude (or length), direction and sense, (i.e., orientation along the given direction.) A _____ is frequently represented by a line segment with a definite direction, or graphically as an arrow, connecting an initial point A with a terminal point B, and denoted by

The magnitude of the _____ is the length of the segment and the direction characterizes the displacement of B relative to A: how much one should move the point A to 'carry' it to the point B.

Chapter 8. Functions of a Complex Variable

Many algebraic operations on real numbers have close analogues for vectors.

a. BDDC
b. Linear partial differential operator
c. 15 theorem
d. Vector

11. In calculus, an antiderivative, primitive or _____ of a function f is a function F whose derivative is equal to f, i.e., F ' = f. The process of solving for antiderivatives is antidifferentiation (or indefinite integration.) Antiderivatives are related to definite integrals through the fundamental theorem of calculus: the definite integral of a function over an interval is equal to the difference between the values of an antiderivative evaluated at the endpoints of the interval.

a. Integral test for convergence
b. Integration by parts operator
c. Arc length
d. Indefinite integral

12. Integration is an important concept in mathematics, specifically in the field of calculus and, more broadly, mathematical analysis. Given a function f of a real variable x and an interval [a, b] of the real line, the _____

$$\int_a^b f(x)\, dx,$$

is defined informally to be the net signed area of the region in the xy-plane bounded by the graph of f, the x-axis, and the vertical lines x = a and x = b.

The term '_____' may also refer to the notion of antiderivative, a function F whose derivative is the given function f.

a. Indefinite integral
b. Integrand
c. Integral
d. Integral test for convergence

13. In mathematics, the _____ of a multivariate differentiable function along a given vector V at a given point P intuitively represents the instantaneous rate of change of the function, moving through P, in the direction of V. It therefore generalizes the notion of a partial derivative, in which the direction is always taken parallel to one of the coordinate axes.

The _____ is a special case of the Gâteaux derivative.

The _____ of a scalar function $f(\vec{x}) = f(x_1, x_2, \ldots, x_n)$ along a vector $\vec{v} = (v_1, \ldots, v_n)$ is the function defined by the limit

<_____> $\nabla_{\vec{v}} f(\vec{x}) = \lim_{h \to 0} \dfrac{f(\vec{x} + h\vec{v}) - f(\vec{x})}{h}.$

Sometimes authors write D_v instead of ∇_v.

a. Linearity of differentiation
b. Directional derivative
c. Differentiation of trigonometric functions
d. Symmetrically continuous

14. In calculus, a branch of mathematics, the _____ is a measurement of how a function changes when its input changes. Loosely speaking, a _____ can be thought of as how much a quantity is changing at some given point. For example, the _____ of the position (or distance) of a vehicle with respect to time is the instantaneous velocity (respectively, instantaneous speed) at which the vehicle is traveling.

The process of finding a _____ is called differentiation. The fundamental theorem of calculus states that differentiation is the reverse process to integration.

a. Bounded function
b. Derivative
c. Semi-differentiability
d. Stationary phase approximation

15. In mathematics, a _____ is an integral where the function to be integrated is evaluated along a curve. Various different line integrals are in use. A specific case of an integration along a closed curve in two dimensions or the complex plane is the contour integral.

a. Radius of convergence
b. Picard theorem
c. Mittag-Leffler star
d. Line integral

16. In mathematics, a _____ is a function whose definition is dependent on the value of the independent variable. Mathematically, a real-valued function f of a real variable x is a relationship whose definition is given differently on disjoint subsets of its domain

The word piecewise is also used to describe any property of a _____ that holds for each piece but may not hold for the whole domain of the function.

a. Range
b. Constant function
c. Surjective
d. Piecewise-defined function

17. For some curves there is a smallest number L that is an upper bound on the length of any polygonal approximation. If such a number exists, then the curve is said to be rectifiable and the curve is defined to have _____ L.

Let C be a curve in Euclidean (or, generally, a metric) space $X = R^n$, so C is the image of a continuous function f : [a, b] → X of the interval [a, b] into X.

a. Integration by parametric derivatives
b. Order of integration
c. Integrand
d. Arc length

18. _____ is the long dimension of any object. The _____ of a thing is the distance between its ends, its linear extent as measured from end to end. This may be distinguished from height, which is vertical extent, and width or breadth, which are the distance from side to side, measuring across the object at right angles to the _____.

a. BDDC
b. 15 theorem
c. BIBO stability
d. Length

Chapter 8. Functions of a Complex Variable

19. Typically the pair u and v are taken to be the real and imaginary parts of a complex-valued function f(x + iy) = u(x,y) + iv (x,y.) Suppose that u and v are continuously differentiable on an open subset of C. Then f = u+iv is holomorphic if and only if the partial derivatives of u and v satisfy the _____ and (1b.)

The equations are one way of looking at the condition on a function to be differentiable (holomorphic) in the sense of complex analysis: in other words they encapsulate the notion of function of a complex variable by means of conventional differential calculus.

a. Viscosity solution
b. Solid harmonics
c. Spherical harmonics
d. Cauchy-Riemann equations

20. In mathematics, the _____ is a representation of a function as an infinite sum of terms calculated from the values of its derivatives at a single point. It may be regarded as the limit of the Taylor polynomials. If the series is centered at zero, the series is also called a Maclaurin series.

a. BDDC
b. BIBO stability
c. 15 theorem
d. Taylor series

21. In mathematics, a (topological) _____ is defined as follows: let I be an interval of real numbers (i.e. a non-empty connected subset of $\mathbb{R}$); then a _____ γ is a continuous mapping $\gamma : I \to X$, where X is a topological space. The _____ γ is said to be simple if it is injective, i.e. if for all x, y in I, we have $\gamma(x) = \gamma(y) \implies x = y$. If I is a closed bounded interval $[a, b]$, we also allow the possibility $\gamma(a) = \gamma(b)$ (this convention makes it possible to talk about closed simple _____.)

a. Closed curve
b. Prolate cycloid
c. Tractrix
d. Curve

22. In mathematics, the _____ of a function y = f(x) is a function that, in some fashion, 'undoes' the effect of f The _____ of f is denoted f⁻¹. The statements y=f(x) and x=f⁻¹(y) are equivalent.

a. ALGOR
b. AUSM
c. ACTRAN
d. Inverse

23. In mathematics, if f is a function from A to B then an _____ for f is a function in the opposite direction, from B to A, with the property that a round trip (a composition) from A to B to A (or from B to A to B) returns each element of the initial set to itself. Thus, if an input x into the function f produces an output y, then inputting y into the _____ f^{-1} (read f inverse, not to be confused with exponentiation) produces the output x. Not every function has an inverse; those that do are called invertible.

a. Inverse function
b. Augustin-Jean Fresnel
c. Augustin Louis Cauchy
d. Aristotle

24. In mathematics, specifically in calculus and complex analysis, the _____ of a function f is defined by the formula

$$\frac{f'}{f}$$

where f' is the derivative of f.

When f is a function f(x) of a real variable x, and takes real, strictly positive values, this is indeed the formula for (log f)', that is, the derivative of the natural logarithm of f, as follows directly from the chain rule.

Many properties of the real logarithm also apply to the _____, even when the function does not take values in the positive reals.

    a. Lin-Tsien equation   b. Logarithmic derivative
    c. Directional derivative   d. Point of inflection

25. A _____ officer is an officer of high military rank. The term or equivalent is used by nearly every country in the world. _____ can be used as a generic term for all grades of _____ officer, or it can specifically refer to a single rank that is just called _____.

    a. BIBO stability   b. 15 theorem
    c. General   d. BDDC

26. In mathematics, the _____ are functions of an angle. They are important in the study of triangles and modeling periodic phenomena, among many other applications. _____ are commonly defined as ratios of two sides of a right triangle containing the angle, and can equivalently be defined as the lengths of various line segments from a unit circle.

    a. Trigonometric functions   b. Sine integral
    c. Trigonometric integrals   d. Trigonometric

27. In mathematics and statistics, the _____ of a list of numbers is the sum of all of the list divided by the number of items in the list. If the list is a statistical population, then the mean of that population is called a population mean. If the list is a statistical sample, we call the resulting statistic a sample mean.

    a. AUSM   b. Arithmetic mean
    c. ALGOR   d. ACTRAN

28. In probability theory and statistics, the _____ (or expectation value or mean and for continuous random variables with a density function it is the probability density -weighted integral of the possible values.

The term '_____' can be misleading.

    a. ACTRAN   b. ALGOR
    c. AUSM   d. Expected value

29. In mathematics, a series (or sometimes also an integral) is said to converge absolutely if the sum (or integral) of the absolute value of the summand or integrand is finite.

More precisely, a real or complex-valued series $\sum_{n=0}^{\infty} a_n$ is said to converge absolutely if $\sum_{n=0}^{\infty} |a_n| < \infty$.

Chapter 8. Functions of a Complex Variable 77

_____ is vitally important to the study of infinite series because on the one hand, it is strong enough that such series retain certain basic properties of finite sums -- the most important ones being rearrangement of the terms and convergence of products of two infinite series -- that are unfortunately not possessed by all convergent series. On the other hand _____ is weak enough to occur very often in practice.

a. ACTRAN
b. Alternating series test
c. Eisenstein series
d. Absolute convergence

30. A _____ of a function of two variables is a curve along which the function has a constant value. In cartography, a _____ (often just called a 'contour') joins points of equal elevation (height) above a given level, such as mean sea level. A contour map is a map illustrated with contour lines, for example a topographic map, which thus shows valleys and hills, and the steepness of slopes.

a. BIBO stability
b. BDDC
c. Contour line
d. 15 theorem

31. In mathematics, the _____ of a power series is a non-negative quantity, either a real number or ∞, that represents a domain (within the radius) in which the series will converge. Within the _____, a power series converges absolutely and uniformly on compacta as well. If the series converges, it is the Taylor series of the analytic function to which it converges inside its _____.

a. Holomorphically separable
b. Branch point
c. Blaschke product
d. Radius of convergence

32. A _____ is a set of standard clothing worn by members of an organization while participating in that organization's activity. Modern uniforms are worn by armed forces and paramilitary organisations such as police, emergency services, security guards, in some workplaces and schools and by inmates in prisons. In some countries, some other officials also wear uniforms in their duties; such is the case of the Commissioned Corps of the United States Public Health Service or the French prefects.

a. ALGOR
b. ACTRAN
c. AUSM
d. Uniform

33. In mathematics, a function f is uniformly continuous if, roughly speaking, it is possible to guarantee that $f(x)$ and $f(y)$ be as close to each other as we please by requiring only that x and y are sufficiently close to each other; unlike ordinary continuity, the maximum distance between $f(x)$ and $f(y)$ cannot depend on x and y themselves. For instance, any isometry (distance-preserving map) between metric spaces is uniformly continuous.

_____, unlike continuity, is meaningless in an arbitrary topological space, since it relies on the ability to compare the sizes of neighbourhoods of distinct points of a space.

a. Uniform continuity
b. ACTRAN
c. AUSM
d. ALGOR

34. In mathematics, a _____ is a series with a constant ratio between successive terms. For example, the series

$$\frac{1}{2} + \frac{1}{4} + \frac{1}{8} + \frac{1}{16} + \cdots$$

is geometric, because each term is equal to half of the previous term. The sum of this series is 1, as illustrated in the following picture:

_____ are one of the simplest examples of infinite series with finite sums.

a. Conditionally convergent
b. Sequence transformation
c. Converge absolutely
d. Geometric series

35. In acoustics and telecommunication, a _____ of a wave is a component frequency of the signal that is an integer multiple of the fundamental frequency. For example, if the fundamental frequency is f, the harmonics have frequencies f, 2f, 3f, 4f, etc. The harmonics have the property that they are all periodic at the fundamental frequency, therefore the sum of harmonics is also periodic at that frequency.

a. BDDC
b. BIBO stability
c. 15 theorem
d. Harmonic

36. In mathematics, mathematical physics and the theory of stochastic processes, a _____ is a twice continuously differentiable function $f : U \to R$ (where U is an open subset of R^n) which satisfies Laplace's equation, i.e.

$$\frac{\partial^2 f}{\partial x_1^2} + \frac{\partial^2 f}{\partial x_2^2} + \cdots + \frac{\partial^2 f}{\partial x_n^2} = 0$$

everywhere on U. This is also often written as

$$\nabla^2 f = 0 \quad \text{or} \quad \Delta f = 0.$$

There also exists a seemingly weaker definition that is equivalent. Indeed a function is harmonic if and only if it is weakly harmonic.

Harmonic functions can be defined on an arbitrary Riemannian manifold, using the Laplace-de Rham operator Δ.

a. Maximum principle
b. Kelvin transform
c. Harmonic function
d. Pluriharmonic function

37. The _____ of an angle is the ratio of the length of the adjacent side to the length of the hypotenuse. In our case

$$\cos A = \frac{\text{adjacent}}{\text{hypotenuse}} = \frac{b}{h}.$$

The tangent of an angle is the ratio of the length of the opposite side to the length of the adjacent side. In our case

$$\tan A = \frac{\text{opposite}}{\text{adjacent}} = \frac{a}{b}.$$

The remaining three functions are best defined using the above three functions.

a. Trigonometric functions
b. Trigonometric
c. Sine integral
d. Cosine

38. In complex analysis, an _____ is a complex-valued function that is holomorphic over the whole complex plane. Typical examples of entire functions are the polynomials, the exponential function, and sums, products and compositions of these. Every _____ can be represented as a power series which converges everywhere, uniformly on compacta.

a. Estimation lemma
b. Identity theorem
c. Analytic continuation
d. Entire function

39. In mathematics, the _____ of a complex function f(z) is a representation of that function as a power series which includes terms of negative degree. It may be used to express complex functions in cases where a Taylor series expansion cannot be applied. The _____ was named after and first published by Pierre Alphonse Laurent in 1843.

a. Laurent series
b. Fundamental recurrence formulas
c. Holomorphic sheaf
d. Riemann surface

40. In mathematics, the _____ (or replacement set) of a given function is the set of 'input' values for which the function is defined. For instance, the _____ of cosine would be all real numbers, while the _____ of the square root would be only numbers greater than or equal to 0 (ignoring complex numbers in both cases.) In a representation of a function in a xy Cartesian coordinate system, the _____ is represented on the x axis (or abscissa.)

a. Domain
b. BIBO stability
c. 15 theorem
d. BDDC

41. In complex analysis, a _____ of a holomorphic function is a point at which the function is ostensibly undefined, but, upon closer examination, the domain of the function can be enlarged to include the singularity (in such a way that the function remains holomorphic.)

For instance, the function

$$f(z) = \frac{\sin z}{z}$$

for z ≠ 0 has a singularity at z = 0. This singularity can be removed by defining f(0) = 1.

a. Maximum modulus principle
b. Mellin inversion formula
c. Logarithmic form
d. Removable singularity

Chapter 8. Functions of a Complex Variable

42. In topology, the boundary of a subset S of a topological space X is the set of points which can be approached both from S and from the outside of S. More formally, it is the set of points in the closure of S, not belonging to the interior of S. An element of the boundary of S is called a _____ of S. S is boundaryless when it contains no boundary, which is to say no _____ Notations used for boundary of a set S include bd(S), fr(S), and ∂S. Some authors (for example Willard, in General Topology) use the term 'frontier', instead of boundary in an attempt to avoid confusion with the concept of boundary used in algebraic topology.

    a. 15 theorem
    b. BIBO stability
    c. Boundary point
    d. BDDC

43. In complex analysis, a mathematical discipline, a _____ of a meromorphic function is a certain type of singularity that behaves like the singularity of $\frac{1}{z^n}$ at z = 0. This means that, in particular, a _____ of the function f(z) is a point z = a such that f(z) approaches infinity uniformly as z approaches a.

Formally, suppose U is an open subset of the complex plane C, a is an element of U and f : U {a} → C is a function which is holomorphic over its domain.

    a. Pole
    b. Bieberbach conjecture
    c. Complex logarithm
    d. Lacunary function

44. In infinitesimal calculus, a _____ is traditionally an infinitesimally small change in a variable. For example, if x is a variable, then a change in the value of x is often denoted Δx (or δx when this change is considered to be small.) The _____ dx represents such a change, but is infinitely small.

    a. Differential
    b. The Method of Mechanical Theorems
    c. Dirichlet integral
    d. Local maximum

45. A _____ is a mathematical equation for an unknown function of one or several variables that relates the values of the function itself and of its derivatives of various orders. they play a prominent role in engineering, physics, economics and other disciplines.

A simplified real world example of a _____ is modeling the acceleration of a ball falling through the air (considering only gravity and air resistance.)

    a. Caloric polynomial
    b. Structural stability
    c. Differential equation
    d. Phase line

46. In complex analysis, an _____ of a function is a 'severe' singularity near which the function exhibits extreme behavior.

Basically, the category _____ is a 'left-over' or default group of singularities that are especially unmanageable: by definition they fit into neither of the other two categories of singularity that be dealt with in some manner - removable singularities and poles

Formally, consider an open subset U in the complex plane C. If there is an element a in U, and a meromorphic function f : U {a} → C.

Chapter 8. Functions of a Complex Variable

a. Estimation lemma
b. Univalent function
c. Argument principle
d. Essential singularity

47. In mathematics, a _____ decomposes a periodic function into a sum of simple oscillating functions, namely sines and cosines (or complex exponentials.) The study of _____ is a branch of Fourier analysis. _____ were introduced by Joseph Fourier (1768-1830) for the purpose of solving the heat equation in a metal plate.

a. 15 theorem
b. BDDC
c. BIBO stability
d. Fourier series

48. In mathematics, a _____ (in one variable) is an infinite series of the form

$$f(x) = \sum_{n=0}^{\infty} a_n (x - c)^n = a_0 + a_1(x - c)^1 + a_2(x - c)^2 + a_3(x - c)^3 + \cdots$$

where a_n represents the coefficient of the nth term, c is a constant, and x varies around c (for this reason one sometimes speaks of the series as being centered at c

In many situations c is equal to zero, for instance when considering a Maclaurin series.

a. Differential coefficient
b. Stationary phase approximation
c. Power series
d. Differential calculus

49. The _____ is a technique for finding approximate solutions to differential equations that is particularly useful in engineering. As of 2005, _____ is the primary analysis technique for computer modeling of mechanical systems as found in structural mechanics.

_____ is related to linear algebra approaches for solving the forces and displacements of a truss.

a. Spring constant
b. Spring equation
c. Navier-Stokes equations
d. Finite element method

50. In geometry, the _____ is a particular mapping (function) that projects a sphere onto a plane. The projection is defined on the entire sphere, except at one point -- the projection point. Where it is defined, the mapping is smooth and bijective.

a. Peirce quincuncial projection
b. Stereographic projection
c. BDDC
d. 15 theorem

51. In complex analysis, the _____ is a complex number which describes the behavior of line integrals of a meromorphic function around a singularity. Residues can be computed quite easily and, once known, allow the determination of more complicated path integrals via the _____ theorem.

The _____ of a meromorphic function f at an isolated singularity a, often denoted Res(f,a) is the unique value R such that $f(z) - \dfrac{R}{(z-a)}$ has an analytic antiderivative in a punctured disk $0 < |z - a| < \delta$.

Chapter 8. Functions of a Complex Variable

    a. Holomorphic sheaf
    b. Picard theorem
    c. Removable singularity
    d. Residue

52. The _____, sometimes called Cauchy's _____, in complex analysis is a powerful tool to evaluate line integrals of analytic functions over closed curves and can often be used to compute real integrals as well. It generalizes the Cauchy integral theorem and Cauchy's integral formula. Illustration of the setting.
    a. Value distribution theory of holomorphic functions
    b. Partial fraction expansion
    c. Maximum modulus principle
    d. Residue theorem

53. In mathematics, the _____ of a closed curve in the plane around a given point is an integer representing the total number of times that curve travels counterclockwise around the point. The _____ depends on the orientation of the curve, and is negative if the curve travels around the point clockwise.

Winding numbers are fundamental objects of study in algebraic topology, and they play an important role in vector calculus, complex analysis, geometric topology, differential geometry, and physics.

    a. 15 theorem
    b. BDDC
    c. BIBO stability
    d. Winding number

54. In integral calculus we would want to write a fractional algebraic expression as the sum of its _____ in order to take the integral of each simple fraction separately. Once the original denominator, D_0, has been factored we set up a fraction for each factor in the denominator. We may use a subscripted D to represent the denominator of the respective _____ which are the factors in D_0.
    a. Left inverse
    b. Closed-form expression
    c. Partial fractions
    d. Multinomial theorem

55. In geometry, the _____ (or simply the tangent) to a curve at a given point is the straight line that 'just touches' the curve at that point (in the sense explained more precisely below.) As it passes through the point of tangency, the _____ is 'going in the same direction' as the curve, and in this sense it is the best straight-line approximation to the curve at that point. The same definition applies to space curves and curves in n-dimensional Euclidean space.
    a. North pole
    b. Lie derivative
    c. Minimal surface
    d. Tangent line

56. In mathematics, a _____ (or critical number) is a point on the domain of a function where:

- one dimension: the derivative (or slope of the line when visualized) is equal to zero or a point where the function ceases to be differentiable.
- in general: there are two distinct concepts: either the derivative (Jacobian) vanishes, or it is not of full rank (or, in either case, the function is not differentiable); these agree in one dimension.

Note that in one dimension, a critical value or critical number x of function f is the domain element at which the derivative is zero or undefined, whereas the associated ordered pair (x, y) is the _____. In higher dimensions a critical value is in the range whereas a _____ is in the domain.

There are two situations in which a point becomes a _____ of a function of one variable. The first of which is that the value of the first derivative is equal to zero.

a. Total derivative
b. Differentiation operator
c. Critical point
d. Multivariable calculus

57. In mathematics, _____ and minima, known collectively as extrema, are the largest value (maximum) or smallest value (minimum), that a function takes in a point either within a given neighbourhood (local extremum) or on the function domain in its entirety (global extremum.)

Throughout, a point refers to an input (x), while a value refers to an output (y): one distinguishing between the maximum value and the point (or points) at which it occurs.

A real-valued function f defined on the real line is said to have a local maximum point at the point x^*, if there exists some $\varepsilon > 0$, such that $f(x^*) \geq f(x)$ when $|x - x^*| < \varepsilon$.

a. Leibniz formula
b. Related rates
c. Maxima
d. Racetrack principle

58. A _____ is an expression which compares quantities relative to each other. The most common examples involve two quantities, but in theory any number of quantities can be compared. In mathematical terms, they are represented by separating each quantity with a colon, for example the _____ 2:3, which is read as the _____ 'two to three'.

a. Sequence
b. Ratio
c. 15 theorem
d. Y-intercept

59. In mathematics, a _____ is the problem of finding a function which solves a specified partial differential equation (PDE) in the interior of a given region that takes prescribed values on the boundary of the region.

The _____ can be solved for many PDEs, although originally it was posed for Laplace's equation. In that case the problem can be stated as follows:

> Given a function f that has values everywhere on the boundary of a region in R^n, is there a unique continuous function u twice continuously differentiable in the interior and continuous on the boundary, such that u is harmonic in the interior and u = f on the boundary?

This requirement is called the Dirichlet boundary condition.

a. Quadrature domain
b. Dirichlet problem
c. Multipole expansion
d. Pluripolar set

60. _____ is the addition of a set of numbers; the result is their sum or total. An interim or present total of a _____ process is termed the running total. The 'numbers' to be summed may be natural numbers, complex numbers, matrices, or still more complicated objects.

a. BIBO stability
b. BDDC
c. 15 theorem
d. Summation

Chapter 8. Functions of a Complex Variable

61. In vector calculus, the _____ is an operator that measures the magnitude of a vector field's source or sink at a given point; the _____ of a vector field is a (signed) scalar. For example, consider air as it is heated or cooled. The relevant vector field for this example is the velocity of the moving air at a point.
   a. Gradient theorem
   b. Triple product
   c. Green's theorem
   d. Divergence

62. In vector calculus a conservative vector field is a vector field which is the gradient of a scalar potential. There are two closely related concepts: path independence and _____ vector fields. Every conservative vector field has zero curl (and is thus _____), and every conservative vector field has the path independence property.
   a. ALGOR
   b. ACTRAN
   c. Irrotational
   d. AUSM

63. In physics, _____ is defined as the rate of change of position. it is vector physical quantity; both speed and direction are required to define it. In the SI (metric) system, it is measured in meters per second: (m/s) or ms^{-1}.
   a. Velocity
   b. BIBO stability
   c. 15 theorem
   d. BDDC

64. In mathematics, a _____ is an ordered list of objects (or events). Like a set, it contains members (also called elements or terms), and the number of terms (possibly infinite) is called the length of the _____. Unlike a set, order matters, and the exact same elements can appear multiple times at different positions in the _____.
   a. 15 theorem
   b. Sequence
   c. Y-intercept
   d. Slope

65. In mathematics a _____ is a construction in vector calculus which associates a vector to every point in a (locally) Euclidean space.

Vector fields are often used in physics to model, for example, the speed and direction of a moving fluid throughout space, or the strength and direction of some force, such as the magnetic or gravitational force, as it changes from point to point.

In the rigorous mathematical treatment, (tangent) vector fields are defined on manifolds as sections of a manifold's tangent bundle.

   a. BDDC
   b. BIBO stability
   c. 15 theorem
   d. Vector field

66. _____ or isopotential in mathematics and physics (especially electronics) refers to a region in space where every point in it is at the same potential. This usually refers to a scalar potential, although it can also be applied to vector potentials. Often, _____ surfaces are used to visualize an (n)-dimensional scalar potential function in (n-1) dimensional space.
   a. Upper convected time derivative
   b. Implicit function theorem
   c. Inverse function theorem
   d. Equipotential

67. In mathematics, the _____ is a fourth-order partial differential equation which arises in areas of continuum mechanics, including linear elasticity theory and the solution of Stokes flows. It is written as

Chapter 8. Functions of a Complex Variable

$$\nabla^4 \varphi = 0$$

where ∇^4 is the fourth power of the del operator and the square of the laplacian operator, and it is known as the biharmonic operator or the bilaplacian operator.

For example, in three dimensional cartesian coordinates the _____ has the form

$$\frac{\partial^4 \varphi}{\partial x^4} + \frac{\partial^4 \varphi}{\partial y^4} + \frac{\partial^4 \varphi}{\partial z^4} + 2\frac{\partial^4 \varphi}{\partial x^2 \partial y^2} + 2\frac{\partial^4 \varphi}{\partial y^2 \partial z^2} + 2\frac{\partial^4 \varphi}{\partial x^2 \partial z^2} = 0.$$

As another example, in n-dimensional Euclidean space,

$$\nabla^4 \left(\frac{1}{r}\right) = \frac{3(15 - 8n + n^2)}{r^5}$$

where

$$r = \sqrt{x_1^2 + x_2^2 + \cdots + x_n^2}.$$

which, for n=3 only, becomes the _____.

a. Biharmonic equation
c. 15 theorem

b. Hopf maximum principle
d. BDDC

Chapter 9. Ordinary Differential Equations

1. In those hierarchically organised churches of Western Christianity which have an ecclesiastical law system, an _____ is an officer of the church who by reason of office has _____ power to execute the church's laws. The term comes from the Latin word ordinarius. In Eastern Christianity, a corresponding officer is called a hierarch, which comes from the Greek word ἱεράρχης meaning 'priestly ruler'.

   a. ACTRAN
   b. Ordinary
   c. AUSM
   d. ALGOR

2. In mathematics, an _____ is a relation that contains functions of only one independent variable, and one or more of its derivatives with respect to that variable.

   A simple example is Newton's second law of motion, which leads to the differential equation

   $$m\frac{d^2x(t)}{dt^2} = F(x(t)),$$

   for the motion of a particle of constant mass m. In general, the force F depends upon the position of the particle x(t) at time t, and thus the unknown function x(t) appears on both sides of the differential equation, as is indicated in the notation F(x(t).)

   a. Implicit differentiation
   b. Implicit function
   c. Automatic differentiation
   d. Ordinary differential equation

3. In geometry, for a finite planar surface of scalar area S, the vector area

   $$\mathbf{S}$$

   is defined as a vector whose magnitude is S and whose direction is perpendicular to the plane, as determined by the right hand rule on the rim (moving one's right hand counterclockwise around the rim, when the palm of the hand is 'touching' the surface, and the straight thumb indicate the direction.)

   $$\mathbf{S} = \hat{\mathbf{n}}S$$

   This can only be defined for flat surfaces, or for regions of curved surfaces which are sufficiently small that they can be considered flat.

   The concept of an _____ simplifies the equation for determining the flux through the surface.

   a. Area vector
   b. ACTRAN
   c. ALGOR
   d. Orthogonal trajectories

4. In infinitesimal calculus, a _____ is traditionally an infinitesimally small change in a variable. For example, if x is a variable, then a change in the value of x is often denoted Δx (or δx when this change is considered to be small.) The _____ dx represents such a change, but is infinitely small.

   a. Dirichlet integral
   b. The Method of Mechanical Theorems
   c. Local maximum
   d. Differential

Chapter 9. Ordinary Differential Equations

5. A _____ is a mathematical equation for an unknown function of one or several variables that relates the values of the function itself and of its derivatives of various orders. they play a prominent role in engineering, physics, economics and other disciplines.

A simplified real world example of a _____ is modeling the acceleration of a ball falling through the air (considering only gravity and air resistance.)

   a. Differential equation   b. Structural stability
   c. Phase line   d. Caloric polynomial

6. In elementary mathematics, physics, and engineering, a _____ is a geometric object that has both a magnitude (or length), direction and sense, (i.e., orientation along the given direction.) A _____ is frequently represented by a line segment with a definite direction, or graphically as an arrow, connecting an initial point A with a terminal point B, and denoted by

The magnitude of the _____ is the length of the segment and the direction characterizes the displacement of B relative to A: how much one should move the point A to 'carry' it to the point B.

Many algebraic operations on real numbers have close analogues for vectors.

   a. Vector   b. 15 theorem
   c. Linear partial differential operator   d. BDDC

7. In calculus, an _____, primitive or indefinite integral of a function f is a function F whose derivative is equal to f, i.e., F >' = f. The process of solving for antiderivatives is antidifferentiation (or indefinite integration.) Antiderivatives are related to definite integrals through the fundamental theorem of calculus: the definite integral of a function over an interval is equal to the difference between the values of an _____ evaluated at the endpoints of the interval.

   a. Antiderivative   b. Indefinite integral
   c. Integrand   d. Order of integration

8. A _____ officer is an officer of high military rank. The term or equivalent is used by nearly every country in the world. _____ can be used as a generic term for all grades of _____ officer, or it can specifically refer to a single rank that is just called _____.

   a. 15 theorem   b. BIBO stability
   c. BDDC   d. General

9. In mathematics, a _____ to an ordinary or partial differential equation is a function for which the derivatives appearing in the equation may not all exist but which is nonetheless deemed to satisfy the equation in some precisely defined sense. There are many different definitions of _____, appropriate for different classes of equations. One of the most important is based on the notion of distributions.

   a. Structural stability   b. Singular perturbation
   c. Conserved quantity   d. Weak solution

Chapter 9. Ordinary Differential Equations

10. In mathematics, an _____ is a theorem with a statement beginning 'there exist(s) ..' y, ... there exist(s) ...'. That is, in more formal terms of symbolic logic, it is a theorem with a statement involving the existential quantifier.
    a. ACTRAN
    b. ALGOR
    c. AUSM
    d. Existence theorem

11. In mathematics, in the field of differential equations, an initial value problem is an ordinary differential equation together with specified value, called the _____, of the unknown function at a given point in the domain of the solution. In physics or other sciences, modeling a system frequently amounts to solving an initial value problem; in this context, the differential equation is an evolution equation specifying how, given initial conditions, the system will evolve with time.

An initial value problem is a differential equation

$$y'(t) = f(t, y(t)) \quad \text{with} \quad f : \mathbb{R} \times \mathbb{R} \to \mathbb{R}$$

together with a point in the domain of f

$$(t_0, y_0) \in \mathbb{R} \times \mathbb{R},$$

called the _____.

   a. ACTRAN
   b. ALGOR
   c. AUSM
   d. Initial condition

12. In mathematics, an _____ or total differential equation is a certain kind of ordinary differential equation which is widely used in physics and engineering.

Given a simply connected and open subset D of R^2 and two functions I and J which are continuous on D then an implicit first-order ordinary differential equation of the form

$$I(x, y)\, dx + J(x, y)\, dy = 0,$$

is called _____ if there exists a continuously differentiable function F, called the potential function, so that

$$\frac{\partial F}{\partial x}(x, y) = I$$

and

$$\frac{\partial F}{\partial y}(x, y) = J.$$

The nomenclature of '_____' refers to the exact derivative (or total derivative) of a function. For a function $F(x_0, x_1, ..., x_{n-1}, x_n)$, the exact or total derivative with respect to x_0 is given by

$$\frac{dF}{dx_0} = \frac{\partial F}{\partial x_0} + \sum_{i=1}^{n} \frac{\partial F}{\partial x_i} \frac{dx_i}{dx_0}.$$

The function

$$F(x, y) := \frac{1}{2}(x^2 + y^2)$$

is a potential function for the differential equation

$$xx' + yy' = 0.$$

In physical applications the functions I and J are usually not only continuous but even continuously differentiable.

a. Integrating factor
b. Exact differential equation
c. Exponential growth
d. Isomonodromic deformation

13. In mathematics, a _____ is a differential equation of the form

$$Ly = f$$

where the differential operator L is a linear operator, y is the unknown function, and the right hand side f is a given function (called the source term.) The linearity condition on L rules out operations such as taking the square of the derivative of y; but permits, for example, taking the second derivative of y. Therefore a fairly general form of such an equation would be

$$a_n(x) D^n y(x) + a_{n-1}(x) D^{n-1} y(x) + \cdots + a_1(x) Dy(x) + a_0(x) y(x) = f(x)$$

where D is the differential operator d/dx (i.e. Dy = y', D^2y = y',...), and the a_i are given functions.

a. Method of undetermined coefficients
b. Petrovsky lacuna
c. Stochastic differential equation
d. Linear differential equation

14. In mathematics, _____ is any of several methods for solving ordinary and partial differential equations, in which algebra allows one to rewrite an equation so that each of two variables occurs on a different side of the equation.

Suppose a differential equation can be written in the form

$$\frac{d}{dx}f(x) = g(x)h(f(x)), \qquad (1)$$

which we can write more simply by letting y = f(x):

$$\frac{dy}{dx} = g(x)h(y).$$

As long as h(y) ≠ 0, we can rearrange terms to obtain:

$$\frac{dy}{h(y)} = g(x)dx,$$

so that the two variables x and y have been separated.

Some who dislike Leibniz's notation may prefer to write this as

$$\frac{1}{h(y)}\frac{dy}{dx} = g(x),$$

but that fails to make it quite as obvious why this is called '_____'.

    a. Damping ratio
    b. Separation of variables
    c. Power series method
    d. Sturm separation theorem

15. _____ is a type of motion in which the velocity of an object changes equal amounts in equal time periods. An example of an object having _____ would be a ball rolling down a ramp. The object picks up velocity as it goes down the ramp with equal changes in time.
    a. Uniform Acceleration
    b. ACTRAN
    c. AUSM
    d. ALGOR

16. In mathematics, constant coefficients is a term applied to differential operators, and also some difference operators, to signify that they contain no functions of the independent variables, other than constant functions. In other words, it singles out special operators, within the larger class of operators having variable coefficients. Such _____ operators have been found to be the easiest to handle, in several respects.
    a. Constant coefficient
    b. Semi-elliptic operator
    c. Dirac operator
    d. Laplacian

17. In mathematics, a _____ is a constant multiplicative factor of a certain object. For example, in the expression $9x^2$, the _____ of x^2 is 9.

The object can be such things as a variable, a vector, a function, etc.

a. Binomial type
b. Resultant
c. Degree of the polynomial
d. Coefficient

18. In mathematics, _____ also known as variation of constants, is a general method to solve inhomogeneous linear ordinary differential equations. It was developed by the Italian-French mathematician Joseph Louis Lagrange with noteworthy help from the American mathematician and physicist Noah LaMoyne.

For first-order inhomogeneous linear differential equations it's usually possible to find solutions via integrating factors or undetermined coefficients with considerably less effort, although those methods are rather heuristics that involve guessing and don't work for all inhomogenous linear differential equations.

a. Variation of parameters
b. Picone identity
c. Phase plane
d. Laser diode rate equations

19. In mathematics, the _____ is a function especially important in the study of differential equations, where it can be used to determine whether a set of solutions is linearly independent.

For n real- or complex-valued functions $f_1, ..., f_n$, which are n >− 1 times differentiable on an interval I, the _____ $W(f_1, ..., f_n)$ as a function on I is defined by

That is, it is the determinant of the matrix constructed by placing the functions in the first row, the first derivative of each function in the second row, and so on through the (n - 1)st derivative, thus forming a square matrix sometimes called a fundamental matrix.

a. BIBO stability
b. BDDC
c. 15 theorem
d. Wronskian

20. In algebra, a _____ is a function depending on n that associates a scalar, det(A), to an n×n square matrix A. The fundamental geometric meaning of a _____ is a scale factor for measure when A is regarded as a linear transformation. Determinants are important both in calculus, where they enter the substitution rule for several variables, and in multilinear algebra.

For a fixed nonnegative integer n, there is a unique _____ function for the n×n matrices over any commutative ring R. In particular, this function exists when R is the field of real or complex numbers.

a. BDDC
b. 15 theorem
c. BIBO stability
d. Determinant

Chapter 9. Ordinary Differential Equations

21. In discrete mathematics, the _____ is used when solving recurrence problems. One can specify a recurrence relation of the form

$$t_n = At_{n-1} + Bt_{n-2}$$

where the value of t_n is dependent on the values of t_{n-1} and t_{n-2}. When solving a recurrence relation, the goal is to eliminate this dependency and derive an equation of the form

$$t_n = c_1 r_1^n + c_2 r_2^n,$$

where c_1 and c_2 are constants and r_1 and r_2 are the roots of the _____

$$r^2 - Ar - B = 0,$$

where A and B are the constants defined in the original recurrence relation.

- a. Sheffer sequence
- b. Leading coefficient
- c. Characteristic equation
- d. Discriminant

22. In acoustics and telecommunication, a _____ of a wave is a component frequency of the signal that is an integer multiple of the fundamental frequency. For example, if the fundamental frequency is f, the harmonics have frequencies f, 2f, 3f, 4f, etc. The harmonics have the property that they are all periodic at the fundamental frequency, therefore the sum of harmonics is also periodic at that frequency.
- a. BIBO stability
- b. 15 theorem
- c. Harmonic
- d. BDDC

23. In mathematics, mathematical physics and the theory of stochastic processes, a _____ is a twice continuously differentiable function f : U → R (where U is an open subset of R^n) which satisfies Laplace's equation, i.e.

$$\frac{\partial^2 f}{\partial x_1^2} + \frac{\partial^2 f}{\partial x_2^2} + \cdots + \frac{\partial^2 f}{\partial x_n^2} = 0$$

everywhere on U. This is also often written as

$$\nabla^2 f = 0 \quad \text{or} \quad \Delta f = 0.$$

There also exists a seemingly weaker definition that is equivalent. Indeed a function is harmonic if and only if it is weakly harmonic.

Harmonic functions can be defined on an arbitrary Riemannian manifold, using the Laplace-de Rham operator Δ.

Chapter 9. Ordinary Differential Equations

a. Kelvin transform
b. Maximum principle
c. Pluriharmonic function
d. Harmonic function

24. A _____ of an oscillating system is a pattern of motion in which all parts of the system move sinusoidally with the same frequency. The frequencies of the normal modes of a system are known as its natural frequencies or resonant frequencies. A physical object, such as a building or a bridge or a molecule, has a set of normal modes that depend on its structure and composition.
a. Boundary value problem
b. Phase plane
c. Power series method
d. Normal mode

25. A curve γ is said to be closed or a loop if $I = [a, b]$ and if $\gamma(a) = \gamma(b)$. A _____ is thus a continuous mapping of the circle S^1; a simple _____ is also called a Jordan curve or a Jordan arc. The Jordan curve theorem states that such curves divide the plane into an 'interior' and an 'exterior'.
a. Curve
b. Bullet-nose curve
c. Kappa curve
d. Closed curve

26. In mathematics, a (topological) _____ is defined as follows: let I be an interval of real numbers (i.e. a non-empty connected subset of $\mathbb{R}$); then a _____ γ is a continuous mapping $\gamma : I \to X$, where X is a topological space. The _____ γ is said to be simple if it is injective, i.e. if for all x, y in I, we have $\gamma(x) = \gamma(y) \implies x = y$. If I is a closed bounded interval $[a, b]$, we also allow the possibility $\gamma(a) = \gamma(b)$ (this convention makes it possible to talk about closed simple _____.)
a. Closed curve
b. Prolate cycloid
c. Curve
d. Tractrix

27. In mathematics, the _____ is a representation of a function as an infinite sum of terms calculated from the values of its derivatives at a single point. It may be regarded as the limit of the Taylor polynomials. If the series is centered at zero, the series is also called a Maclaurin series.
a. BDDC
b. BIBO stability
c. 15 theorem
d. Taylor series

28. Integration is an important concept in mathematics, specifically in the field of calculus and, more broadly, mathematical analysis. Given a function f of a real variable x and an interval [a, b] of the real line, the _____

$$\int_a^b f(x)\, dx,$$

is defined informally to be the net signed area of the region in the xy-plane bounded by the graph of f, the x-axis, and the vertical lines x = a and x = b.

The term '_____' may also refer to the notion of antiderivative, a function F whose derivative is the given function f.

a. Integral test for convergence
b. Integral
c. Integrand
d. Indefinite integral

Chapter 10. Partial Differential Equations

1. Typically the pair u and v are taken to be the real and imaginary parts of a complex-valued function f(x + iy) = u(x,y) + iv (x,y.) Suppose that u and v are continuously differentiable on an open subset of C. Then f = u+iv is holomorphic if and only if the partial derivatives of u and v satisfy the _____ and (1b.)

The equations are one way of looking at the condition on a function to be differentiable (holomorphic) in the sense of complex analysis: in other words they encapsulate the notion of function of a complex variable by means of conventional differential calculus.

a. Solid harmonics
b. Cauchy-Riemann equations
c. Viscosity solution
d. Spherical harmonics

2. In acoustics and telecommunication, a _____ of a wave is a component frequency of the signal that is an integer multiple of the fundamental frequency. For example, if the fundamental frequency is f, the harmonics have frequencies f, 2f, 3f, 4f, etc. The harmonics have the property that they are all periodic at the fundamental frequency, therefore the sum of harmonics is also periodic at that frequency.

a. 15 theorem
b. BIBO stability
c. BDDC
d. Harmonic

3. In mathematics, mathematical physics and the theory of stochastic processes, a _____ is a twice continuously differentiable function f : U → R (where U is an open subset of R^n) which satisfies Laplace's equation, i.e.

$$\frac{\partial^2 f}{\partial x_1^2} + \frac{\partial^2 f}{\partial x_2^2} + \cdots + \frac{\partial^2 f}{\partial x_n^2} = 0$$

everywhere on U. This is also often written as

$$\nabla^2 f = 0 \quad \text{or} \quad \Delta f = 0.$$

There also exists a seemingly weaker definition that is equivalent. Indeed a function is harmonic if and only if it is weakly harmonic.

Harmonic functions can be defined on an arbitrary Riemannian manifold, using the Laplace-de Rham operator Δ.

a. Kelvin transform
b. Maximum principle
c. Harmonic function
d. Pluriharmonic function

4. In infinitesimal calculus, a _____ is traditionally an infinitesimally small change in a variable. For example, if x is a variable, then a change in the value of x is often denoted Δx (or δx when this change is considered to be small.) The _____ dx represents such a change, but is infinitely small.

a. Local maximum
b. The Method of Mechanical Theorems
c. Differential
d. Dirichlet integral

5. A _____ is a mathematical equation for an unknown function of one or several variables that relates the values of the function itself and of its derivatives of various orders. they play a prominent role in engineering, physics, economics and other disciplines.

A simplified real world example of a _____ is modeling the acceleration of a ball falling through the air (considering only gravity and air resistance.)

    a. Structural stability
    c. Differential equation
    b. Phase line
    d. Caloric polynomial

6. In vector calculus a _____ vector field (also known as an incompressible vector field) is a vector field v with divergence zero:

$$\nabla \cdot \mathbf{v} = 0.$$

The fundamental theorem of vector calculus states that any vector field can be expressed as the sum of a conservative vector field and a _____ field. The condition of zero divergence is satisfied whenever a vector field v has only a vector potential component, because the definition of the vector potential A as:

$$\mathbf{v} = \nabla \times \mathbf{A}$$

automatically results in the identity (as can be shown, for example, using Cartesian coordinates):

$$\nabla \cdot \mathbf{v} = \nabla \cdot (\nabla \times \mathbf{A}) = 0.$$

The converse also holds: for any _____ v there exists a vector potential A such that $\mathbf{v} = \nabla \times \mathbf{A}$.

The divergence theorem, gives the equivalent integral definition of a _____ field; namely that for any closed surface S, the net total flux through the surface must be zero:

$$\iint_S \mathbf{v} \cdot d\mathbf{s} = 0$$

where $d\mathbf{s}$ is the outward normal to each surface element.

    a. Trigonometric series
    c. Principal part
    b. Bloch space
    d. Solenoidal

7. A quantity is said to be subject to _____ if it decreases at a rate proportional to its value. Symbolically, this can be expressed as the following differential equation, where N is the quantity and λ is a positive number called the decay constant.

$$\frac{dN}{dt} = -\lambda N.$$

Chapter 10. Partial Differential Equations

The solution to this equation is:

$$N(t) = N_0 e^{-\lambda t}.$$

Here N(t) is the quantity at time t, and N_0 = N(0) is the initial quantity, i.e. the quantity at time t = 0.

a. Exponential sum
b. Exponential decay
c. ALGOR
d. ACTRAN

8. In mathematics, the hyperbolic functions are analogs of the ordinary trigonometric functions. The basic hyperbolic functions are the hyperbolic sine 'sinh', and the _____ 'cosh', from which are derived the hyperbolic tangent 'tanh', etc., in analogy to the derived trigonometric functions. The inverse hyperbolic functions are the area hyperbolic sine 'arsinh' (also called 'asinh', or sometimes by the misnomer of 'arcsinh') and so on.
   a. Hyperbolic cosine
   b. Step function
   c. Hyperbolic tangent
   d. Square root function

9. A curve γ is said to be closed or a loop if $I = [a, b]$ and if $\gamma(a) = \gamma(b)$. A _____ is thus a continuous mapping of the circle S^1; a simple _____ is also called a Jordan curve or a Jordan arc. The Jordan curve theorem states that such curves divide the plane into an 'interior' and an 'exterior'.
   a. Curve
   b. Kappa curve
   c. Bullet-nose curve
   d. Closed curve

10. In mathematics, a (topological) _____ is defined as follows: let I be an interval of real numbers (i.e. a non-empty connected subset of $\mathbb{R}$); then a _____ γ is a continuous mapping $\gamma : I \to X$, where X is a topological space. The _____ γ is said to be simple if it is injective, i.e. if for all x, y in I, we have $\gamma(x) = \gamma(y) \implies x = y$. If I is a closed bounded interval $[a, b]$, we also allow the possibility $\gamma(a) = \gamma(b)$ (this convention makes it possible to talk about closed simple _____.)
    a. Tractrix
    b. Prolate cycloid
    c. Closed curve
    d. Curve

11. In computer science and information science, _____ could also be a method or an algorithm. Again, an example will illustrate: There are systems of counting, as with Roman numerals, and various systems for filing papers, or catalogues, and various library systems, of which the Dewey Decimal _____ is an example. This still fits with the definition of components which are connected together (in this case in order to facilitate the flow of information.)
    a. BDDC
    b. BIBO stability
    c. 15 theorem
    d. System

12. In discrete mathematics, the _____ is used when solving recurrence problems. One can specify a recurrence relation of the form

$$t_n = A t_{n-1} + B t_{n-2}$$

where the value of t_n is dependent on the values of t_{n-1} and t_{n-2}. When solving a recurrence relation, the goal is to eliminate this dependency and derive an equation of the form

$$t_n = c_1 r_1^n + c_2 r_2^n,$$

where c_1 and c_2 are constants and r_1 and r_2 are the roots of the _____

$$r^2 - Ar - B = 0,$$

where A and B are the constants defined in the original recurrence relation.

a. Characteristic equation
b. Discriminant
c. Sheffer sequence
d. Leading coefficient

13. A _____ of an oscillating system is a pattern of motion in which all parts of the system move sinusoidally with the same frequency. The frequencies of the normal modes of a system are known as its natural frequencies or resonant frequencies. A physical object, such as a building or a bridge or a molecule, has a set of normal modes that depend on its structure and composition.

a. Power series method
b. Boundary value problem
c. Phase plane
d. Normal mode

14. _____ is any effect, either deliberately engendered or inherent to a system, that tends to reduce the amplitude of oscillations of an oscillatory system.

In physics and engineering, _____ may be mathematically modelled as a force synchronous with the velocity of the object but opposite in direction to it. If such force is also proportional to the velocity, as for a simple mechanical viscous damper (dashpot), the force F may be related to the velocity v by

$$\mathbf{F} = -c\mathbf{v}$$

where c is the viscous _____ coefficient, given in units of newton-seconds per meter.

a. BDDC
b. 15 theorem
c. BIBO stability
d. Damping

15. _____ can be thought of as energy stored within a physical system. It is called _____ because it has the potential to be converted into other forms of energy, such as kinetic energy, and to do work in the process. The standard (SI) unit of measure for _____ is the joule, the same as for work or energy in general.

a. Law of Conservation of Energy
b. BDDC
c. Potential energy
d. 15 theorem

Chapter 10. Partial Differential Equations

16. The _____ of an object is the extra energy which it possesses due to its motion. It is defined as the work needed to accelerate a body of a given mass from rest to its current velocity. Having gained this energy during its acceleration, the body maintains this _____ unless its speed changes.
   a. 15 theorem
   b. Law of Conservation of Energy
   c. BDDC
   d. Kinetic energy

17. In mathematics, an _____ space is a vector space with the additional structure of _____. This additional structure associates each pair of vectors in the space with a scalar quantity known as the _____ of the vectors. Inner products allow the rigorous introduction of intuitive geometrical notions such as the length of a vector or the angle between two vectors.
   a. ALGOR
   b. ACTRAN
   c. Inner product
   d. AUSM

18. In mathematics, two vectors are _____ if they are perpendicular, i.e., they form a right angle. For example, a subway and the street above, although they do not physically intersect, are _____ if they cross at a right angle.
   a. ALGOR
   b. Orthogonal
   c. ACTRAN
   d. AUSM

19. In mathematics and its applications, a _____ system is a system for assigning an n-tuple of numbers or scalars to each point in an n-dimensional space. This concept is part of the theory of manifolds. 'Scalars' in many cases means real numbers, but, depending on context, can mean complex numbers or elements of some other commutative ring.
   a. Cylindrical coordinate system
   b. Coordinate
   c. Spherical coordinate system
   d. 15 theorem

20. The _____ of an angle is the ratio of the length of the adjacent side to the length of the hypotenuse. In our case

$$\cos A = \frac{\text{adjacent}}{\text{hypotenuse}} = \frac{b}{h}.$$

The tangent of an angle is the ratio of the length of the opposite side to the length of the adjacent side. In our case

$$\tan A = \frac{\text{opposite}}{\text{adjacent}} = \frac{a}{b}.$$

The remaining three functions are best defined using the above three functions.

   a. Trigonometric functions
   b. Trigonometric
   c. Sine integral
   d. Cosine

21. In mathematics, an _____ space is a topological space whose dimension is n (where n is a fixed natural number.) The archetypical example is _____ Euclidean space, which describes Euclidean geometry in n dimensions.

Many familiar geometric objects can be generalized to any number of dimensions.

100 Chapter 10. Partial Differential Equations

    a. BIBO stability
    c. 15 theorem
    b. N-dimensional
    d. BDDC

22. The _____ of an angle is the ratio of the length of the opposite side to the length of the hypotenuse. In our case

$$\sin A = \frac{\text{opposite}}{\text{hypotenuse}} = \frac{a}{h}.$$

Note that this ratio does not depend on size of the particular right triangle chosen, as long as it contains the angle A, since all such triangles are similar.

The cosine of an angle is the ratio of the length of the adjacent side to the length of the hypotenuse.

    a. Trigonometric functions
    c. Sine integral
    b. Sine
    d. Trigonometric

23. In elementary mathematics, physics, and engineering, a _____ is a geometric object that has both a magnitude (or length), direction and sense, (i.e., orientation along the given direction.) A _____ is frequently represented by a line segment with a definite direction, or graphically as an arrow, connecting an initial point A with a terminal point B, and denoted by

$\boxed{\times}\,$>

The magnitude of the _____ is the length of the segment and the direction characterizes the displacement of B relative to A: how much one should move the point A to 'carry' it to the point B.

Many algebraic operations on real numbers have close analogues for vectors.

    a. Linear partial differential operator
    c. Vector
    b. 15 theorem
    d. BDDC

24. In differential geometry there are a number of second-order, linear, elliptic differential operators bearing the name _____

The connection _____ is a differential operator acting on the various tensor bundles of a manifold, defined in terms of a Riemmanian- or pseudo-Riemannian metric.

    a. Dirac operator
    c. Semi-elliptic operator
    b. Peetre theorem
    d. Laplacian

25. The _____ is an important second-order linear partial differential equation that describes the propagation of a variety of waves, such as sound waves, light waves and water waves. It arises in fields such as acoustics, electromagnetics, and fluid dynamics. Historically, the problem of a vibrating string such as that of a musical instrument was studied by Jean le Rond d'Alembert, Leonhard Euler, Daniel Bernoulli, and Joseph-Louis Lagrange.

a. Lagrangian
b. Wave equation
c. Dirac equation
d. Volume

26. In mathematics, in the field of differential equations, an initial value problem is an ordinary differential equation together with specified value, called the _____, of the unknown function at a given point in the domain of the solution. In physics or other sciences, modeling a system frequently amounts to solving an initial value problem; in this context, the differential equation is an evolution equation specifying how, given initial conditions, the system will evolve with time.

An initial value problem is a differential equation

$$y'(t) = f(t, y(t)) \quad \text{with} \quad f : \mathbb{R} \times \mathbb{R} \to \mathbb{R}$$

together with a point in the domain of f

$$(t_0, y_0) \in \mathbb{R} \times \mathbb{R},$$

called the _____.

a. ALGOR
b. AUSM
c. Initial condition
d. ACTRAN

27. _____ is the long dimension of any object. The _____ of a thing is the distance between its ends, its linear extent as measured from end to end. This may be distinguished from height, which is vertical extent, and width or breadth, which are the distance from side to side, measuring across the object at right angles to the _____.
a. BDDC
b. 15 theorem
c. BIBO stability
d. Length

28. In physics, _____ is defined as the rate of change of position. it is vector physical quantity; both speed and direction are required to define it. In the SI (metric) system, it is measured in meters per second: (m/s) or ms^{-1}.
a. BIBO stability
b. BDDC
c. Velocity
d. 15 theorem

29. In mathematics, an _____ is a function that is locally given by a convergent power series. Analytic functions can be thought of as a bridge between polynomials and general functions. There exist both real analytic functions and complex analytic functions, categories that are similar in some ways, but different in others.
a. Imaginary number
b. Euler's formula
c. Upper half-plane
d. Analytic function

30. In mathematics, _____ also known as variation of constants, is a general method to solve inhomogeneous linear ordinary differential equations. It was developed by the Italian-French mathematician Joseph Louis Lagrange with noteworthy help from the American mathematician and physicist Noah LaMoyne.

For first-order inhomogeneous linear differential equations it's usually possible to find solutions via integrating factors or undetermined coefficients with considerably less effort, although those methods are rather heuristics that involve guessing and don't work for all inhomogenous linear differential equations.

a. Variation of parameters
c. Picone identity
b. Laser diode rate equations
d. Phase plane

31. In mathematics, a _____ is a constant multiplicative factor of a certain object. For example, in the expression $9x^2$, the _____ of x^2 is 9.

The object can be such things as a variable, a vector, a function, etc.

a. Degree of the polynomial
c. Resultant
b. Binomial type
d. Coefficient

32. In mathematics, in the field of differential equations, a _____ is a differential equation together with a set of additional restraints, called the boundary conditions. A solution to a _____ is a solution to the differential equation which also satisfies the boundary conditions.

Boundary value problems arise in several branches of physics as any physical differential equation will have them.

a. Spectral theory of ordinary differential equations
c. Boundary value problem
b. Variation of parameters
d. Mathieu functions

33. In mathematics, a _____ decomposes a periodic function into a sum of simple oscillating functions, namely sines and cosines (or complex exponentials.) The study of _____ is a branch of Fourier analysis. _____ were introduced by Joseph Fourier (1768-1830) for the purpose of solving the heat equation in a metal plate.

a. 15 theorem
c. Fourier series
b. BDDC
d. BIBO stability

34. In mathematics, specifically in calculus and complex analysis, the _____ of a function f is defined by the formula

$$\frac{f'}{f}$$

where f' is the derivative of f.

When f is a function f(x) of a real variable x, and takes real, strictly positive values, this is indeed the formula for (log f)', that is, the derivative of the natural logarithm of f, as follows directly from the chain rule.

Many properties of the real logarithm also apply to the _____, even when the function does not take values in the positive reals.

a. Directional derivative
c. Point of inflection
b. Lin-Tsien equation
d. Logarithmic derivative

35. In mathematics, _____ is any of several methods for solving ordinary and partial differential equations, in which algebra allows one to rewrite an equation so that each of two variables occurs on a different side of the equation.

Chapter 10. Partial Differential Equations

Suppose a differential equation can be written in the form

$$\frac{d}{dx}f(x) = g(x)h(f(x)), \qquad (1)$$

which we can write more simply by letting y = f(x):

$$\frac{dy}{dx} = g(x)h(y).$$

As long as h(y) ≠ 0, we can rearrange terms to obtain:

$$\frac{dy}{h(y)} = g(x)dx,$$

so that the two variables x and y have been separated.

Some who dislike Leibniz's notation may prefer to write this as

$$\frac{1}{h(y)}\frac{dy}{dx} = g(x),$$

but that fails to make it quite as obvious why this is called '_____'.

a. Power series method
c. Damping ratio

b. Sturm separation theorem
d. Separation of variables

36. In calculus, a branch of mathematics, the _____ is a measurement of how a function changes when its input changes. Loosely speaking, a _____ can be thought of as how much a quantity is changing at some given point. For example, the _____ of the position (or distance) of a vehicle with respect to time is the instantaneous velocity (respectively, instantaneous speed) at which the vehicle is traveling.

The process of finding a _____ is called differentiation. The fundamental theorem of calculus states that differentiation is the reverse process to integration.

a. Stationary phase approximation
c. Semi-differentiability

b. Bounded function
d. Derivative

37. In mathematics, a _____ is the problem of finding a function which solves a specified partial differential equation (PDE) in the interior of a given region that takes prescribed values on the boundary of the region.

The _____ can be solved for many PDEs, although originally it was posed for Laplace's equation. In that case the problem can be stated as follows:

> Given a function f that has values everywhere on the boundary of a region in R^n, is there a unique continuous function u twice continuously differentiable in the interior and continuous on the boundary, such that u is harmonic in the interior and u = f on the boundary?

This requirement is called the Dirichlet boundary condition.

a. Multipole expansion
c. Pluripolar set
b. Quadrature domain
d. Dirichlet problem

38. Integration is an important concept in mathematics, specifically in the field of calculus and, more broadly, mathematical analysis. Given a function f of a real variable x and an interval [a, b] of the real line, the _____

$$\int_a^b f(x)\,dx,$$

is defined informally to be the net signed area of the region in the xy-plane bounded by the graph of f, the x-axis, and the vertical lines x = a and x = b.

The term '_____' may also refer to the notion of antiderivative, a function F whose derivative is the given function f.

a. Integral
c. Integral test for convergence
b. Indefinite integral
d. Integrand

39. _____ is a field of mathematics that deals with functionals, as opposed to ordinary calculus which deals with functions. Such functionals can for example be formed as integrals involving an unknown function and its derivatives. The interest is in extremal functions: those making the functional attain a maximum or minimum value.

a. First variation
c. Hu-Washizu principle
b. Variational vector field
d. Calculus of variations

40. In mathematics, _____ and minima, known collectively as extrema, are the largest value (maximum) or smallest value (minimum), that a function takes in a point either within a given neighbourhood (local extremum) or on the function domain in its entirety (global extremum.)

Throughout, a point refers to an input (x), while a value refers to an output (y): one distinguishing between the maximum value and the point (or points) at which it occurs.

A real-valued function f defined on the real line is said to have a local maximum point at the point x^*, if there exists some $\varepsilon > 0$, such that $f(x^*) \geq f(x)$ when $|x - x^*| < \varepsilon$.

a. Related rates
c. Maxima
b. Racetrack principle
d. Leibniz formula

41. The _____ is, in quantum mechanics, one way of finding approximations to the lowest energy eigenstate or ground state, and some excited states. The basis for this method is the variational principle.

Suppose we are given a Hilbert space and a Hermitian operator over it called the Hamiltonian H. Ignoring complications about continuous spectra, we look at the discrete spectrum of H and the corresponding eigenspaces of each eigenvalue λ :

$$\sum_{\lambda_1, \lambda_2 \in \text{Spec}(H)} \langle \psi_{\lambda_1} | \psi_{\lambda_2} \rangle = \delta_{\lambda_1 \lambda_2}$$

where $\delta_{i,j}$ is the Kronecker delta

$$\hat{H} |\psi_\lambda\rangle = \lambda |\psi_\lambda\rangle.$$

a. Perturbation theory
c. 15 theorem
b. Ritz method
d. Variational method

42. The _____ is a technique for finding approximate solutions to differential equations that is particularly useful in engineering. As of 2005, _____ is the primary analysis technique for computer modeling of mechanical systems as found in structural mechanics.

_____ is related to linear algebra approaches for solving the forces and displacements of a truss.

a. Spring equation
c. Finite element method
b. Navier-Stokes equations
d. Spring constant

43. In applied mathematics and mechanical engineering, the _____ is a widely used, classical method for the calculation of the natural vibration frequency of a structure in the second or higher order. It is a direct variational method in which the minimum of a functional defined on a normed linear space is approximated by a linear combination of elements from that space. This method will yield solutions when an analytical form for the true solution may be intractable.

a. Rayleigh-Ritz method
c. 15 theorem
b. BIBO stability
d. BDDC

44. In mathematics, a _____ (or critical number) is a point on the domain of a function where:

- one dimension: the derivative (or slope of the line when visualized) is equal to zero or a point where the function ceases to be differentiable.
- in general: there are two distinct concepts: either the derivative (Jacobian) vanishes, or it is not of full rank (or, in either case, the function is not differentiable); these agree in one dimension.

Note that in one dimension, a critical value or critical number x of function f is the domain element at which the derivative is zero or undefined, whereas the associated ordered pair (x, y) is the _____. In higher dimensions a critical value is in the range whereas a _____ is in the domain.

There are two situations in which a point becomes a _____ of a function of one variable. The first of which is that the value of the first derivative is equal to zero.

a. Differentiation operator
b. Total derivative
c. Multivariable calculus
d. Critical point

45. In mathematical optimization, the method of Lagrange multipliers provides a strategy for finding the maximum/minimum of a function subject to constraints.

For example, consider the optimization problem

$$\text{maximize } f(x, y)$$
$$\text{subject to } g(x, y) = c.$$

We introduce a new variable (λ) called a _____, and study the Lagrange function defined by

$$\Lambda(x, y, \lambda) = f(x, y) - \lambda\Big(g(x, y) - c\Big).$$

If (x,y)‰ is a maximum for the original constrained problem, then there exists a λ such that (x,y,λ)‰ is a stationary point for the Lagrange function (stationary points are those points where the partial derivatives of Λ are zero.) However, not all stationary points yield a solution of the original problem.

a. BIBO stability
b. 15 theorem
c. BDDC
d. Lagrange multiplier

46. In numerical mathematics, the _____ is a method for obtaining numerical approximations to the solutions of systems of equations, including certain types of elliptic partial differential equations, in particular Laplace's equation and its generalization, Poisson's equation. The function is assumed to be given on the boundary of a shape, and has to be computed on its interior.

This _____ should not be confused with the unrelated relaxation technique in mathematical optimization.

a. Hyperstability
b. Streamline diffusion
c. Relaxation method
d. Higher-order derivative test

ANSWER KEY

Chapter 1
1. c   2. c   3. c   4. d   5. d   6. c   7. d   8. d   9. d   10. d
11. d 12. c 13. c 14. d 15. d 16. d 17. b 18. b 19. a 20. c
21. d 22. d 23. d

Chapter 2
1. b   2. a   3. d   4. d   5. a   6. b   7. a   8. d   9. d   10. d
11. a 12. d 13. d 14. d 15. d 16. c 17. d 18. c 19. a 20. b
21. b 22. a 23. b 24. a 25. b 26. c 27. d 28. d 29. c 30. d
31. c 32. b 33. c 34. d 35. d 36. d 37. d 38. d 39. d 40. d
41. d 42. d 43. a 44. a 45. c 46. d 47. d 48. d 49. c 50. d
51. d 52. c 53. b 54. b

Chapter 3
1. c   2. a   3. d   4. d   5. a   6. d   7. a   8. d   9. d   10. d
11. c 12. b 13. c 14. a 15. a 16. d 17. d 18. d 19. b 20. b
21. b 22. a 23. a 24. c 25. c 26. b

Chapter 4
1. c   2. d   3. d   4. c   5. d   6. d   7. d   8. d   9. a   10. d
11. d 12. d 13. c 14. d 15. c 16. b 17. a 18. c 19. b 20. b
21. d 22. c 23. d 24. d 25. d 26. d 27. a 28. b 29. d 30. a
31. b 32. b

Chapter 5
1. b   2. c   3. c   4. d   5. c   6. a   7. d   8. a   9. d   10. d
11. a 12. d 13. b 14. c 15. d 16. b 17. a 18. a 19. d 20. b
21. d 22. d 23. a 24. b 25. d 26. a 27. a 28. d 29. c 30. c
31. a 32. c 33. a 34. d 35. b 36. a 37. b 38. d 39. d 40. b
41. c

Chapter 6
1. c   2. c   3. d   4. c   5. d   6. c   7. d   8. d   9. d   10. a
11. d 12. d 13. c 14. b 15. b 16. b 17. d 18. d 19. d 20. d
21. a 22. a 23. c 24. c 25. d 26. a 27. d 28. d 29. b 30. d
31. b 32. d 33. b 34. d 35. b 36. d 37. c 38. c 39. b 40. d
41. d 42. b 43. a 44. d 45. d 46. d 47. d 48. a

Chapter 7
1. d   2. a   3. d   4. a   5. d   6. d   7. d   8. d   9. d   10. c
11. a 12. d 13. d 14. d 15. c 16. c 17. d 18. d 19. d 20. a
21. b 22. a 23. d 24. c 25. b 26. d 27. d 28. c 29. d 30. a
31. d 32. d 33. d 34. b 35. d 36. d 37. a 38. a

Chapter 8

1. d	2. d	3. d	4. b	5. c	6. a	7. a	8. c	9. a	10. d
11. d	12. c	13. b	14. b	15. d	16. d	17. d	18. d	19. d	20. d
21. d	22. d	23. a	24. b	25. c	26. a	27. b	28. d	29. d	30. c
31. d	32. d	33. a	34. d	35. d	36. c	37. d	38. d	39. a	40. a
41. d	42. c	43. a	44. a	45. c	46. d	47. d	48. c	49. d	50. b
51. d	52. d	53. d	54. c	55. d	56. c	57. c	58. b	59. b	60. d
61. d	62. c	63. a	64. b	65. d	66. d	67. a			

Chapter 9

1. b	2. d	3. a	4. d	5. a	6. a	7. a	8. d	9. d	10. d
11. d	12. b	13. d	14. b	15. a	16. a	17. d	18. a	19. d	20. d
21. c	22. c	23. d	24. d	25. d	26. c	27. d	28. b		

Chapter 10

1. b	2. d	3. c	4. c	5. c	6. d	7. b	8. a	9. d	10. d
11. d	12. a	13. d	14. d	15. c	16. d	17. c	18. b	19. b	20. d
21. b	22. b	23. c	24. d	25. b	26. c	27. d	28. c	29. d	30. a
31. d	32. c	33. c	34. d	35. d	36. d	37. d	38. a	39. d	40. c
41. d	42. c	43. a	44. d	45. d	46. c